THE HORSE'S MOUTH

As a director, Mervyn Millar's work includes: *Evidence for the Existence of Borrowers* on tour (Total Theatre Award, Herald Angel Award); *Yellow Lines* at Oval House; *School of Dark* for Apples and Snakes; *The Baba Yaga* at BAC; *At Home, North Hill Relay, Elevation* and *The Lusiads* all for wireframe; and *On Line and Paranoid in the Sentimental City* (Pearson Award), *Man Is Man, The National Theatre, Final Call, The Optimist's Daughters,* and *Cells* all at the Finborough Theatre, where he was Director. As co-director: *The Wonderful Life and Miserable Death of the Renowned Magician Doctor Faustus* for NT Education; and *Unfolding Andersen* for Theatre-Rites/British Library. As puppetry director: *The Comedy of Errors* for the RSC; *Great Expectations* for the RSC/Cheek by Jowl; *The Magic Carpet* and *The Odyssey* at the Lyric Hammersmith; *Macbeth* and *The Little Tempest* for NT Education; *Around the World in Eighty Days* at Liverpool Playhouse; and *Jason and the Argonauts, Uncle Ebenezer,* and *The Sound of Music* at BAC. As assistant director: *Tall Horse* for Handspring (international tour); and *Shopworks* for Theatre-Rites (LIFT/Theater der Welt festival). His previous book, *Journey of the Tall Horse,* about Handspring's *Tall Horse*, is also published by Oberon.

Mervyn Millar
The Horse's Mouth
Staging Morpurgo's *War Horse*

Published in 2007 by the National Theatre
in association with Oberon Books Ltd

National Theatre, South Bank, London SE1 9PX
www.nationaltheatre.org.uk/publications

Oberon Books
521 Caledonian Road, London N7 9RH
info@oberonbooks.com
www.oberonbooks.com

ISBN 1 84002 765 7 / 978 1 84002 765 5

Photographs by Simon Annand and Mervyn Millar

Puppetry designs by Adrian Kohler

Cover design based on Michael Mayhew's NT poster

Back cover photograph (Luke Treadaway with Joey as a foal) by Simon Annand

Inside cover drawings by Rae Smith

Other books in the 'National Theatre at Work' series are: Robert Butler's
Humble Beginnings, *Just About Anything Goes*, *The Art of Darkness* and
The Alchemist Exposed; Jonathan Croall's *Hamlet Observed*, *Inside the
Molly House*, and *Peter Hall's Bacchai*; and Bella Merlin's *With the Rogue's
Company*. Di Trevis' *Remembrance of Things Proust* also explores the process
of putting on a play at the National.

Series editor Lyn Haill

Series © The National Theatre 2006

Printed in Great Britain by Antony Rowe Ltd, Chippenham.

Contents

Introduction

Tom Morris phoned up and said that they had this novel, about the War Horse. He said, 'It's the story of a horse, who goes through the war: and the war is seen through the eyes of the horse. There's a love story between the horse and the boy from the farm. The horse doesn't take sides, because it's a horse, and so it's a very clever device to look at war dispassionately.'
I thought, that sounds like a great idea.

Adrian Kohler

IN 2005 I WAS WORKING with Handspring Puppet Company in South Africa on their epic touring production *Tall Horse*, the true story of a giraffe that travelled from the Sudan to Paris. *Tall Horse* featured complex and intricate puppets, performing alongside actors and musicians. Tom Morris was one of my mentors on the Arts Council Bursary that had taken me there. Tom is an Associate Director at the National Theatre, and was formerly the Artistic Director of BAC, South London's thriving space for emerging theatre, where we had worked together. Tom and the NT's Executive Director Nick Starr appeared in Cape Town when *Tall Horse* was playing, combining a trip to look at my progress, size up venues for touring the NT's production of *Primo*, and look over *Tall Horse*. This ambitious co-production between Handspring (one of South Africa's leading theatre companies) and the celebrated Sogolon puppet troupe from Mali in West Africa had been in development for several years. It blended two very different African cultures in a show that took a wry look at Enlightenment Europe's civilization. The making of *Tall Horse* is told in 'Journey of the Tall Horse', to which this book is in part a sequel.

As Handspring's Adrian Kohler says, "I've known him [Tom Morris] since we performed *Faustus* at the Battersea Arts Centre, and he's been interested in working with us: I think he saw something unusual in the *Faustus*, and something intriguing in the hyena in that production, and it must have sat in the back of his mind for a while." Handspring's *Faustus in Africa!* (which visited the UK in 1995) was the second in a trilogy of very successful collaborations with the South African artist and theatre-maker William Kentridge: European legends transplanted to Africa, given contemporary political edge, and produced using a thrilling combination of actors, carved wooden puppets, charcoal animation and a battery of sound and lighting.

The result of the visit was not an invitation for the spectacular *Tall Horse*, with its complement of over 80 puppets including several antelope and a four-metre high giraffe, to visit the NT, but something bolder and braver – an invitation to explore a new project that would bring together the National Theatre's Literary and Studio departments in collaboration with these phenomenal puppet designers.

Tom Morris thought he had found a story for them to tell. Michael Morpurgo's *War Horse* is a much-loved children's book, translated into 35 languages around the world, and shortlisted for the Whitbread prize.

The National Theatre had a gap to fill. Alongside the rest of its programme of classics and new plays, the NT wants to secure a new audience. The National's Director Nicholas Hytner grabbed the attention of young people with his two-part production of *His Dark Materials*, Philip Pullman's epic trilogy, in 2003 and 2004. As he observes, "It's a brilliant audience to engage and it's important it's engaged. Otherwise there won't be an audience tomorrow." These shows don't duplicate the NT's Education department's work, of making theatre accessible to young audiences. They sit in the repertoire and make the link between young adults and the large space of the Olivier. Tom Morris stresses the quality of the productions: "Since *His Dark Materials*, the National has been very interested in making shows which are accessible to that audience age-range and which don't compromise on production values. This is the third, after *His Dark Materials* and *Coram Boy*."

This book has been written by combining private interviews with members of the company with remarks made in the workshop and rehearsal room, and setting them all in my memory of our intentions when it was happening. It may sometimes seem as if the work was constant over the two years of development – and of course, in our heads, some of it was. But the main work took place in three workshops at the National Theatre Studio: for a week in January 2005, for three weeks in June 2006, and for three-and-a half weeks in March 2007. Handspring worked with designer Rae Smith for a short week in November 2006 which led up to a meeting with the directors (coincidentally, on armistice day). There have been countless script and planning meetings in addition. I've been privileged to have contributed to the piece from the first workshops – and in the condensation to a short book, I hope I've remembered most of it right.

I'd like to have written more about everything in the development of the show – the emergence of the video language, Adrian Sutton's work on the score and how Chris Shutt and Paule Constable have added their ingenuity and artistry to the rehearsal room work. I'd like to have said more about how stage management and the dedicated departments in the building (wardrobe, wigs, the armoury, props) mobilise to fulfil the demands that emerge from the rehearsal room – but while there's no limit to how much I could tell you, there's a limit to how long a book of this type should be. The timescale of printing and producing the book also means that it will be finished before rehearsals are – so I'm not able to tell you as much about the characters of the actors in rehearsal, and the camaraderie and ideas that emerge there, as I'd like. I hope I haven't spent a lot of space discussing moments that might get cut or altered radically in late rehearsal, technical rehearsal or previews.

The book is dedicated to the memory of Fourie Nyamande. Fourie was an actor and puppeteer, and a member of Handspring Puppet Company, who should have been in *War Horse*, but sadly he died in late 2006. I first met Fourie first when he was touring Europe in his first production with Handspring, *The Chimp Project*, in 2000. Basil and Adrian were convinced they had found someone special – and they were right. Fourie committed with enormous joy and seriousness to what he did, and managed that rarest of combinations in a performer – to be brimmingly exuberant and technically precise at the same time. The fact that he could effortlessly fill a stage was the more marked by the fact that he also knew how to disappear into anonymity behind a puppet. Fourie was humble and genuine in his relationships and took on both his work and life with a finely-judged mixture of humour and seriousness. It's telling that the reason he died was because he kept his sickness quiet while his partner was in hospital giving birth to their first child. *War Horse* is a play all about the loss of loved ones, and for us, one of those is Fourie.

MM

1. War and Peace

When I heard they wanted to do it, I thought: they're mad. I mean, how can you tell a serious story about horses, on stage, in front of a serious audience?

Michael Morpurgo

WAR HORSE IS THE STORY of a horse. In the novel by Michael Morpurgo, a horse is forcefully separated from its mother and auctioned to a Devon farmer. The horse grows up with a farm boy called Albert. They form a friendship and Albert names the horse Joey. But they are separated when Joey is bought by the Army as war is declared on Germany in 1914. After two disastrous cavalry actions, our horse is one of two captured by the German army and put to work pulling, first an ambulance, and subsequently a heavy gun. During their time behind German lines, the horses are loved by a young girl, Emilie, and protected by a soldier called Friedrich. But as the British army advance, Joey's companion Topthorn dies of exhaustion, and, running from a tank, Joey escapes from both armies. A panicked flight leaves him in no-man's land, where, by the toss of a coin, he is reclaimed by the British. In need of medical attention, Joey finds Albert by chance, and they nurse each other back to health. Their connection is threatened again when the army attempt to auction their horses in France rather than bring them back – but the family of dead Emilie outbids the butchers, and gives the horse to Albert once again.

Perhaps the most extraordinary of all the extraordinary things about the book *War Horse* is that it is written entirely from the horse's point of view. Human beings come and go, and it's the perspective of Joey that guides the reader through the appalling horrors of the First World War. As Morpurgo says, "My plot for the book really was to tell that story through the eyes of the horse but to go right the way through the war." He took on this artistic and technical challenge with relish: "Historically one thing I think we're all told is: you don't make animals talk, let alone write a book, because it's a very, very risky thing to do; if you get it wrong, it simply is ridiculous… [but] knowing that there had been books written before, where an animal tells a tale, you know it can be done."

And as Rae Smith, the designer of the National Theatre's adaptation of the book, affirms, Morpurgo pulls it off:

The play comes from a book that's a real page-turner. You rip through it really quickly. And you're very excited by the emotional engagement of the horse and his heartfelt relationships with human beings.

Rae, her directors Tom Morris and Marianne Elliott, writer Nick Stafford, their collaborators Handspring Puppet Company, and their creative team, have taken on the task of turning this page-turner into an epic production for the Olivier Theatre, the largest of the National Theatre's three auditoriums, with its wide sweep of audience arranged around an open, circular stage.

But how do you start in adapting a story about a horse? And how did writer Nick Stafford tackle the always tricky process of compressing and re-imagining a prose work as a piece of drama?

War Horse the play starts with Tom Morris, an associate director at the NT. He tells me that he was tipped off to the book by his mother. He'd been looking at Morpurgo's work with a view to possible adaptations, but she pointed him in the direction of this unique story about a horse. "I knew immediately who to approach," he says: the celebrated South African puppet company Handspring. As Morris continues:

The first thing or notion in place, was how the lead character was going to be portrayed. And that, basically, is how the project grew from reading the book.

There are plenty of ways in which the horse might have been portrayed. Morris, who has as good an acquaintance as anyone in the country with experimental, physical and visual theatre styles, from his time as Artistic Director of BAC, knows most of them. But the most exciting to him was the language of puppetry. Puppet theatre is not everyone's cup of tea. And, as Adrian Kohler of Handspring observes, "I think the people who don't like puppet theatre will always not like it. There are quite a few of those. And a lot of people think puppet theatre's not sexy. But, amongst us who do," he adds, "I think we have a growing audience." He refers to "the gift of the story: an inarticulate animal has been given centre stage." To him, "It has to be a puppet, and in a mainstream production of this kind, it's quite a unique project."

The National Theatre doesn't usually run a star system: although celebrated actors are sometimes a selling point for a production, it's more frequent that the script, or the simple ambition of a project, will be the reason for producing it. The National's bold two-part staging of *His Dark Materials* in 2003 and 2004 made extensive use of puppets, but they never looked to an animal as the central focus. For *War Horse*, Morris and Handspring have decided that at the centre of it all will be a puppet horse.

The process of 'writing' *War Horse* began in 2005 in a short workshop at the National Theatre Studio. Different writers had been attached to the project across the early workshop discussions, but in 2006 the literary department and Morris made the decision to work with Nick Stafford. Stafford has written plays for theatres all over the country: Birmingham, Northampton, Hampstead, the Royal Shakespeare Company, and the acclaimed *Battle Royal* for the NT in 1999. He's a solid, tough-looking man, shaven-headed and reserved, but even a small amount of work with him reveals a tender, careful and sensitive character. Stafford isn't demonstrative or dramatic; and the creative team of *War Horse* is in general a group who expend their energy on the work rather than on themselves.

The first decision is that the horse on stage will not speak. Stafford explains:

> *This story is told, by Michael Morpurgo, via a horse's view of the world. We've shifted from the first-person to the third: that's a big change, and the horse is not speaking.*

As Adrian Kohler says:

> *To put a horse speaking on the stage is… well, a little bit Disney, perhaps. You would be saying, well, is it really a person? It would anthropomorphise the horse too much. So here's the challenge of the piece: to see if the horse can be articulate without speaking.*

If the most extraordinary thing about the central character of *War Horse* is that it is a horse, then anything that happens on stage to make it less of a horse makes Morpurgo's story less bold. With the paperback in hand, a reader can make the distinction between what a horse is conscious of and what is happening around the horse. On stage the audience member can do the same. For the horse to address the audience would be comical, and to hear a human voice expressing the horse's thoughts would undermine that special perspective. So the challenge for the production is to make a horse that the audience can identify with, and to leave space in the script for the horse to communicate with the audience without speaking. Co-director Marianne Elliott outlines the way the story functions:

The main character is the catalyst that drives everything but doesn't speak. And that's this horse.

As Stafford puts it, "Joey's in the war without knowing what it is." Joey understands nothing of the war, or of politics, or of the rivalry, friendship and conflict of human society. He takes a journey through the play – he's the only constant presence – and his decisions and actions alter and illuminate the behaviour of the humans around him. There are two theatrical challenges facing Stafford: writing for a puppet, and writing for a character that doesn't speak.

The decision to lose the horse's viewpoint is a bold one, but it's not the viewpoint itself that is at the heart of Morpurgo's intention:

If the book works, it works because of the aim behind the voice: and that aim is to be able to listen to the voices of British soldiers, German soldiers, French civilians, so that you see the war through their eyes and through the horse's eyes at the same time – if it is powerful, it's because of the intention behind it.

On stage, everything happens in the third person, to many characters at once. However much the director might focus the action on a speech by a single character, members of the audience are free to pay attention to the third soldier listening to it. Except where events are narrated directly to the audience by the only visible character, the playwright is unable to restrict the audience's perspective in the way a novelist might.

One of the most memorable passages in the book comes in the first cavalry action in France, when Nicholls is, shockingly, shot from his mount. Morpurgo's use of perspective is compelling – the horse's back is one of its few blind spots, and so Joey's sensation is of sound, and of the weight of Nicholls being lifted from his back – a beautifully understated sequence, elegant and minimal. On stage, the event of Nicholls being blown off the back of a horse has a very different effect – it's a spectacular set-piece. With something as visually extraordinary as this happening, it's impossible to keep the focus inside Joey's head, as Morpurgo is able to do on the page.

"The book is not easy to turn into a play," says Kohler, "because it's a journey, the horse is meeting many different characters, and as the horse doesn't speak, how do you sustain the drama through the piece?" As National Theatre Director Nicholas Hytner warns, "The toughest thing that they've got to achieve is a theatre structure that is compelling, tense and involving from beginning to end. There is no getting around the fact that for a large-scale piece of populist theatre, which sets out to engage as many people as possible, a well-structured, tense, and involving narrative is an absolute necessity." And with this in mind, the team set about building a narrative structure around the events in the book. The first step of this, drawn up a full two years before the first performance, was a 13-page breakdown of the action created by Tom Morris, following the plotting of the book and proposing scenes suitable for dramatisation.

An essential part of Stafford's task in making any play is to populate the stage with characters. Morpurgo's Nicholls is only what Joey describes of him: the Olivier audience's version of him, to be played by an actor, needs to be more fully explored: "The humans," notes Stafford, "only exist via the horse in the book. They have to take on completely independent lives, and to be, more or less, created." Because Joey will not be explaining what's happening, as Marianne Elliott says, "you have to fill out the story, because, if other characters are going to tell it, rather than the horse, then they have to live as three-dimensional characters, rather than impressions the horse has."

Morpurgo's restriction of perspective means he can make the characters instantly memorable, and they stand out boldly on reading the book: Stewart and Nicholls, the contrasting officers Joey meets on the British side; drunken Ted Narracott; crazy Friedrich on the German side. "It's good for us," says Stafford, "that there are some really strong characters in the book." It's necessary for Stafford to build vivid prose vignettes into complex, lasting through-lines. He expands characters to give them more time in the eyes of the audience, so that they have their own developing stories in the background of Joey's journey. He adds a few of his own, like Sergeant Thunder, who guides the troops when they arrive at Calais. But "every major event and character originates from the book," he says.

One difficulty is to keep hold of Albert while we are simultaneously following Joey. In the book, Joey is able to remember Albert; but our puppet horse's thoughts aren't shared, and we find ourselves seeing the war from Albert's point of view too. This bond is one of the reasons for our strong feelings for both characters. As Morpurgo explains:

Affection for an animal can be very intense, for children growing up on a farm alone. This boy's affection for this foal, who he comes across and looks after – and let's remember, he was an only child – represents the kind of friendship and respect that develop between a country boy, a country girl, and the animals around.

In the novel, Marianne Elliott remembers, "the love story between Albert and Joey was really compelling." On stage, this side of Albert's story is combined with his own journey through the war – the character distinguished in both stories with what Stafford describes as "absolute single-minded loyalty and devotion".

The knot of *War Horse*'s action takes that bond into the First World War. In the book, a horse's eye-view allows the war to be seen in flashes and glimpses. A stage production will also show the war around the horse – and as the team look to show the passing of time between scenes, it becomes appropriate to look at how much of the war the play is aiming to present. Morris affirms that "it's very important that it does tell that story," but as Elliott puts it, the play "functions viscerally as a portrait of the war. It's by no means a historical portrait – or even necessarily a fair portrait."

But the war is crucial to the story, of course. As Morpurgo puts it: "When I wrote *War Horse*, I was very interested in writing a story which somehow expressed the universal suffering that went on in war." For Morris, "this show certainly isn't a tragedy about the suffering of animals in war. The point about it is that the horse is a perfect witness to the human experiences of war on both sides." It's no mistake that Morpurgo's horse goes from being a free horse, to a British, to a German, to a British horse again, without feeling any change. Joey sees patriots, cowards, anti-war activists and heroes, and witnesses a range of attitudes from the bullish to the maudlin on both sides. Elliott continues the thought: "we're trying to tell a story which is about humans in a situation, and you like, or dislike, or have complicated feelings about those people because they're humans – not because they're German or English." So the task is to use the linear story of one horse's experience to shed light on the experience of those around him – and to use the horse's pure neutrality to restrain any tendency towards distorting the picture. Morpurgo confirms that this is perhaps the most important thread in his conception:

I want no-one to come out of the play, or indeed finish the book, thinking that it is about winning a war. Above everything it is about how every single side suffers.

"It's one of those things you grow up with isn't it, if you're English?" says Nick Stafford about the First World War. "You think you know about it, and then you realise that you didn't at all. I am amazed at how little I know. This project has made me really have to learn what happened." During the workshops, Stafford became our expert on the war. While all of us read and researched widely, Stafford was able to discuss with confidence the structure of a cavalry regiment, the most likely channel ports for departure and arrival, or the journey a wounded soldier might go on from clearing station to military hospital, with informed speculation on which parts of the journey might involve horses. And even more, he had to research the systems on both sides of the trenches: whilst British military protocol may be easier to get information on, Joey spends the bulk of the war with the German army. I asked Stafford if he was writing about war in general. "I'm writing about this specific war," he replied. "There may be some general things about war you can draw from that, but it is specifically this war." Any play that takes real events into its compass has a responsibility, and Stafford and his directors take their responsibility to the truth seriously.

• • •

The adaptation process started with Tom Morris' 13-page synopsis. "I gave him [Stafford] a treatment for the script," says Morris, "and said, 'This is how I think the story might go, please take it on from here.' I explained that because of the nature of the project it was going to be a collaborative process and I was going to be interfering; and he said, 'Yes, I understand, that's the nature of the beast, it's a bit like a film. Let's go.' And he's been absolutely fantastically flexible from the off." One of Stafford's first observations after he'd produced his first draft was how the play falls into a five-act structure. All of the first act has Joey as a young foal. Act 2 shows Joey grown in Devon, facing trials and bonding with Albert. In Act 3 Joey is in the British army, in Act 4 he's on the German side, and Act 5 has the reunion with Albert. This initial sketch for the structure has served us in good stead. It emphasises how the story of Joey is bigger than the story of the war; that we are interested in forging Joey and Albert's relationship through their struggles in peacetime; that the war breaks that relationship up and it's only as it ends that they can come together. Stafford perceives this as one of the key articles of faith to Morpurgo's vision: "It has to be about Joey and Albert meeting, falling in love, being separated, and finding each other again. I think those things are immutable."

"The war will have a different type of storytelling to the home," warned Stafford at the beginning of 2007. It's a crucial point, and it frees us all up to look at how it's possible to show anything of the enormous horror of the war when it's seen in glimpses. He doesn't shy away from it – there sometimes seem to be deaths in every scene of the war section. At different times he works on offering different facets of wartime experience, focusing on how each character fights a war, or gets though a war, on realistic expectations of the conflict and on the fading ideals of those fighting.

Stafford's work rate and focus are extraordinary. He produces a series of drafts and half-drafts, often delivering new pages halfway through a workshop day as he seizes on the opportunity to give shape to an idea that has emerged in the rehearsal room. As the first schematic draft develops into fuller explorations of the characters, the teams begin to feel the effect of Stafford's work. Handspring's Basil Jones says of the third draft: "I felt a whole world of emotion, rippling and vibrating... the whole feels like an emotional organism." Marianne Elliott was wryer in her encouragement: "The writing has a lot more Nick Stafford in it." The really tough part of the writing process is in the editing.

At a read-through before the March 2007 workshop that runs to two-and-a-half hours, Elliott estimates a length of four hours with all the visual sequences included. We're aiming for under three, including the interval. The pressure is on to find ways of compressing the action. Stafford, Elliott and Morris are aware of two essential needs: to find the threads of symbolism, character and mood that will lead the audience through the story; and to be unsentimental in the work of removing sections that hold up the pace or become redundant to a stage version of the story. The rehearsal draft is number 8.5 – and Stafford is still on hand during rehearsals, amending, adjusting, and providing rewrites as necessary.

From the middle of 2006, doubts are emerging about whether the French auction at the end of the war has enough to sustain an audience who have just watched the emotional reunion of Albert and Joey. It's the beginning of the discussion about whether to end the story sooner than Morpurgo does in the novel. This decision springs from a desire to make a satisfying shape for the end of the evening in the theatre, but it has ramifications backward in the story – if we don't have this event, then what is the purpose of the young girl, Emilie? Morris and Handspring have always had an instinct that Emilie will be a human character played by a puppet. This suggests that her role in the stage production is more than narrative; she carries a symbolic charge, offers a shorthand to the audience that she and Joey share an innocence and simplicity that exists outside the difficult wartime social politics that affect her mother or the soldiers. Emilie is able to remind us what Albert was like before he entered the war. These changes develop the character of Emilie for the stage production; even more than other characters, her role in the stage version alters from that in the book – and her character grows and emerges to fit.

Stafford's research suggests that, as the regiment would have been drawn from one local area, Trooper Warren, the third of Joey's riders, might also have lived in or around Albert's village in Devon. The creative team accept this opportunity fully, extending Warren's story right back to provide a contrasting adolescent to Albert. Warren acquires a first name, Ned, and a father; and the story of the Narracotts' Devon life develops very quickly, via strong contrasts, into a reflection of the pressures on a rural Edwardian farming family. At a late stage, the script conferences between Morris, Elliott and Stafford bring a new complexity and depth to these scenes when the Warrens become Ted Narracott's in-laws: as well as being rivals for Joey, Ned and Albert are sparring cousins, and Ted's hostility to Warren acquires extra spice as a family feud. Other characters who need to have vivid life in the minds of the audience become combined too: one example is the Hauptmann who captures Joey and Topthorn. The decision to combine him with their protector, the sympathetic 'mad German', Friedrich, results in the creation of a major character who will guide us through the horses' experience of the War; and savage Karl, who forces the horses to pull his artillery piece, also has his life extended backwards to be another of the German soldiers who capture Ned and Stewart – his savagery to the horses later is more expected after an audience have seen his brutal stabbing of young Ned.

Something unexpected happens with the character of Major Nicholls (transformed from a Captain in the novel to accommodate his status in the regiment). There's no decision or explicit desire to build up the character or stage time of Nicholls; indeed, he stays on stage initially because Morpurgo's story offers the arresting image of him lodged in a tree after the first disastrous cavalry action – and once you've put an actor in a tree, it's no bad thing to let that image loom over the next couple of scenes before the interval. But Morpurgo wrote his book inspired by a picture of a horse, and Nicholls is the man who draws that picture of Joey. In such a visually-literate creative team, the picture of the horse was perhaps bound to gain a special status. Nicholls draws Joey into history, and in our version, his sketchbook offers us an introduction to the world of Devon in the play. In France, hung in his tree, his body observes the rest of the war. At different times in the script discussions he is offered, by various members of the team, as a war poet; as the leader of a chorus of the dead who observe the war; as a prophet who foretells the effect of machine-guns, or is troubled by visions of Joey in jeopardy. Nicholls makes a connection with Joey that's almost as strong as Albert's; and he makes a connection with Albert too. He's introduced just as the story makes its decisive change of gear, from its foundations in Devon into the unknown territory of the war. As we head into rehearsals, he stays with Albert into the hell of his war. Nicholls, and his sketchbook, seem to haunt the creative team meetings as much as they do Albert on stage. He becomes another of our threads through the play.

And as the drafts keep coming, Albert's war becomes better defined. Early scenes in which he is on patrol, in no-man's-land and almost as disoriented as Joey, evolve into a definite and specific sense of direction. As Morris observes of the fourth draft, "There's a sense of Albert getting closer to where Joey is." Stafford works to locate the action of Joey's and Albert's wars, mapping out how their experience fits in with the historical development of the war. So we know that Joey goes over to German lines in February 1915, and we can chart the advance of Albert's regiment in 1918 towards recognisable territory – and characters – that we associate with Joey. It means that Emilie's farm is a physical reference point for the audience during the unfolding of the 1915–18 years, and eventually results in a scene between Albert and Emilie – two characters that, unknown to each other, have both cared for the same horse – that none of the writers would have been bold enough to propose. It has emerged from separate ideas for scenes that best tell the story of Albert and Joey's progress, and the need to keep them grounded in specific reality. Morpurgo is in contact with this replotting process. As he presents it shortly before rehearsals start, "I'm not a dramatist, I'm not a dramaturg. What has been lovely about the business with the National has been that Tom Morris has, right from the start, asked me 'what do I think, what do I think, what do I think, about this...' Now, in fact, I'm making comments on the seventh draft. And it's wonderful, because I've seen the way the weaving of this script is coming together, relationships beginning to make great sense, and the unravelling of the story becoming more intense."

"I've not just enjoyed it," Morpurgo goes on, "I've found it enormously stimulating as a writer, because it enables you to revisit work that you've done... it's lovely working with people who come to it with a fresh head and a fresh pair of eyes and are turning it in a different direction and translating it into another form. We're looking not at something that replicates, but at something that extends the story, deepens the story, hardens the story even."

The nature of the collaboration in shaping the storytelling makes this adaptation far from a one-man job. For example, at a meeting in late February 2007, in advance of the upcoming workshop, the creative team attempt to plot through our current understanding of how the scenes are to be staged, but while Nick Stafford is keenly observant, he's largely silent. With these visual storytellers responding to his latest draft, he prefers to listen to them. And when the team discuss and shape a scene like the ploughing, which is about a horse and a boy's non-verbal communication, they are writing the play just as much as Stafford is.

A point of reference since the earliest workshops has been horse-whispering, the influential school of training made famous by Monty Roberts, which stresses the need to communicate with the horse on its own terms. It seems to correlate with the trusting relationship that Albert builds up with Joey – contrasted with the clumsier horsemanship of his father or Ned Warren. The company enthusiastically take in the videos and books of Roberts and his disciples' methods. They're great guides to how someone might or might not behave well with a horse, and they also provide charming stage images – an actor in the second workshop ends up stretched on the floor trying to gain the horse's trust without facing him square on.

Improvisations with the horse and actors in workshops create scenes for Stafford to write, but also scenes in which the critical action happens alongside the words. And as Joey's relationships with people continue throughout the play, this level of the storytelling comes into its own. As Albert learns what's comfortable for Joey, we hope the audience will too; and as the other characters relate to the horse in their own way, this visual language becomes something that Nick Stafford needs to weave into his script. It's more than a matter of knowing that it's happening – in a big space like the Olivier, visual storytelling is an asset. Stafford needs to make sure that the rhythm and flow of his scenes allow time and space for these developing relationships to occupy the audience's attention. It means that it's essential for him to watch them in action. And when a puppet Emilie or Topthorn interacts with a puppet Joey, there's little for Stafford to write in the script except what the audience is to perceive from the movement.

There are other visual sequences than those concerned with puppetry, and other languages for Stafford to take on. Some are literal. From the first workshops, the team have a feeling that it might strengthen our identification with Joey if the soldiers on the German side spoke real German, rather than accented English. It would mean that for the (predominantly) non-German speaking audience, a large section of the second half of the play would contain only fragments of understandable dialogue. It would mean that the principal language of storytelling becomes, not the literary one of speeches, but a visual one. Our main way of understanding relationships between the actors will be through their physical behaviour – just as we read that of the horses, and just as the horses themselves read the situation. We'll enter the mind of the horse a little more, and we will be attuned to this way of reading the action because of the emphasis on puppetry. The movement of puppets is one of their strongest means of communication.

Rae Smith's design features a large screen for projecting images and shadow puppetry. In combination with the large stage space, it offers all sorts of possibilities for conjuring imagery and locations. These languages will come into their own in describing the big story arc – the movement of place and of time. And when the scene-by-scene story of Joey's war skips across the years, the screen and stage will offer ways of telling something of the story of war that Stafford, Morris and Elliott feel necessary. It seems to me that some sense of this epic scale is good for a production in the Olivier – it matches the scale of the space, and relates the figure of the individual actor to the world he or she is in.

In this case, that world is a world of war, and as the workshops and meetings progress, ideas for telling the story of war come from all members of the team: it's ensemble writing. 'Passage of time' sequences, which include a number of these ideas, are designed to move fluidly between stage and screen – to create an interplay of actors' movement, silhouette image, and drawn and filmed material that might enable the focus of the audience to be continually moving around the theatre. The attention and interpretation of the audience knit the various sources of information together to make the story live in the space. That's the hope, anyway.

Morris very often works as Stafford's partner in filtering and assessing the contributions, and weighing them against the demands of the space, with Elliott keeping a sharp eye on the clarity and logic of the storytelling. As Adrian Kohler reflects, "It's been a fascinating process to see how the script's been tackled. How the demands of the production are presented to Nick and the kind of polite but firm way with which Tom goes about it. Nick Stafford has been amazing in his flexibility on that level, but I think Tom has been incredibly reasonable in his demands and Nick has understood them."

2. The National Theatre at Work

Of all of the projects I've ever worked on at the National Theatre, I think this is the most... I would like to use another word than 'organic', because that's so old fashioned, but it's the most process-based. The experience of making the world together actually turns up on stage. It's more like an art project than a theatre project.

Rae Smith

"**THE NATIONAL THEATRE, HISTORICALLY,**" says Tom Morris, "has been, like most British theatres, in the business of delivering scripts to the audience through production. And," he adds, in understatement, "that's not what we're doing." When theatre-makers don't know how to do something, they need to try it out. One of the places they go to do it, especially if they work at the NT, is the National Theatre Studio, a vital resource to the theatre since its formation in 1984. Morris is a large, enthusiastic man who beams his enjoyment so visibly that he often seems a little like an untended, overgrown child. His role in our work is very frequently to ask questions, and very frequently the question he asks is "What if we did this?" Morris is at the heart of *War Horse*: from his first hunch that it might be possible, right through to the last drafting when he's still pushing for stronger, bolder, theatrical solutions, and into rehearsals, endlessly trying to knot together image, story and music. One of his great abilities is to confront his collaborators' natural caution and deliberately, gently erode it: to invite them to test what they can do.

"As long as you are working at the limits of what you can, and pushing what you do further," says Adrian Kohler, "then that's the best you can do. If you present something like that

to an audience then surely that work will show through."
One thing that bonds the work of the *War Horse* team is a
willingness to face the limits of what they know how to do,
and step out beyond. It makes the experience an exciting and
sometimes frightening one, and it means that it's all the more
likely that *War Horse* will offer the audience something that
they haven't seen before.

The head of the National Theatre Studio is Purni Morell. "The
Studio really exists to answer questions that the National Theatre
might have," she says. "Either about a specific project or about
theatre in general. It's a place that various departments from
the National Theatre will use as a resource to work out projects
that they have ongoing."

Tom Morris is able to be more specific to *War Horse*:

*This project would have been absolutely impossible
without the Studio. What the Studio sometimes does
is support the development of work in a pre-rehearsal
stage. In this case, in order to work out how to tell a story
in the Olivier – which has always been understood as a
theatre for text-based work – with a puppet in the central
role, and for the central role to be non-speaking, it was
absolutely essential to spend some time... arsing around
in the Studio, basically.*

The Studio doesn't make a very visible impact on the public,
and Purni Morell stresses how important this is. "It's private: it
has no public element whatsoever. It's a place where you can
go and pursue your investigation and take from it what you
want, without the pressure of any other kind of expectation."
The work at the Studio is invisible; but the courage it allows,
and the ideas it helps deliver, are fully visible on the NT's stages
and on other stages around the country. When *War Horse*
started its development, the head of Studio was Lucy Davies.

She recalls that "We didn't do anything else in my time that involved such sophisticated making, and puppets on this scale. The lead in *War Horse* poses unique challenges, and we hadn't done a collaboration with a company on another continent, so moments to connect and share work were really invaluable." For Handspring's Basil Jones, who always works with visual storytelling, workshopping time is an integral part of the development of any project. "I think it's essential," he says, "to allow projects to breathe before they take their first breath on stage."

In March 2007, *War Horse*'s third major workshop begins with a read-through of the latest script. Everyone's here: in addition to the core creatives, there are production and stage management, sound designer Chris Shutt, Leo Warner & Mark Grimmer from video designers FiftyNine Productions Ltd, staff director Polly Findlay, Allan Edwards from the NT's props department, and seven or eight actors, all in the Education department's portakabin opposite the rear of the main NT building. Tom Morris makes the introduction, which is telling – this is the first public presentation since he officially took the role of co-director alongside Marianne Elliott. "We've set ourselves the ridiculous challenge of making a show for the Olivier where the central character is a horse who does not speak," he says mildly. He also introduces a new language to us: "There will also be a strong element in the show of song."

"The job of this workshop is," he goes on, "for us as a group to get our heads around the story and see how text and image are combining. With something like this, you don't know till you see it whether it works or not." He and Elliott unveil their ambitious plan: to try to create a rough staging, however ramshackle, of the whole script, in only a fortnight.

A bit later in the year, Morris looks back affectionately on our first workshop in January 2005, "when we had the unadorned human horse." The 'unadorned human horse' was the beginning of an exploration of how little we might need to represent a horse on stage. Morris, Kohler and Jones wanted to try out a range of solutions, from a single actor, to a pair of actors, and then adding in parts of puppets: horse masks, hooves, horses' heads, simple manes and tails, examining which elements did enough to convey horse-ness to an audience. The actors in that workshop, Toby Sedgwick, Helena Lymbery, Ed Woodall and Sam Barnett, had little puppetry experience, but plenty in physical theatre. Sedgwick has worked with most of the major British physical theatre companies since leaving the famous Jacques Lecoq school in Paris and founding his own company, The Moving Picture Mime Show. He's provided movement direction to many theatres up and down the country and was at the heart of Morris's emergent team.

Right from the beginning, it was clear that Morris believes in full involvement. Everyone needs to be ready to get up and do something in his workshops. It's unusual for Basil Jones and Adrian Kohler not to be on stage in their shows, but they planned not to perform in *War Horse*. Yet they and I were as likely to be stamping and snorting in the workshop room as Sedgwick or Lymbery.

The focus of that first workshop was mainly on representing horses, and being enthused about the novel itself. Tom had made the first steps towards his breakdown of a structure, but for him and for Handspring, this workshop was about questioning their assumptions. Handspring make extraordinary, complex animal puppets – but would they need to? The knowledge of how much horse-ness was available from the actors alone underpinned much of the later development work.

The second main workshop, in 2006, had something more concrete to work from: a first draft by Nick Stafford. The script was a set of first rough drafts of scenes, many of them those proposed by Morris. The other draft was the prototype horse, built in Cape Town by Adrian Kohler and shipped by sea to London.

There are no rules for how a piece might be developed in the Studio. Morris and Elliott have different perspectives and different strategies for pursuing their individual goals, but one of our most important tasks was to find out, and to demonstrate to Elliott and Stafford, what the prototype horse could do. Meanwhile, Elliott always wants to examine the latest draft of the script, and to test the relationships and connections thoroughly. As she says, "You've got to make sure that each line is warranted and is motivated for the character; and that each important moment's in the proper place, and the structure works." Elliott frequently focuses on clarifying and amplifying psychological subtext, restarting the scene and inviting the actors to take clearer and bolder objectives into the situation that Stafford or Morpurgo's writing provides. The process emphasises what's most crucial to the characters and gives Stafford ideas on how he might have them behave.

And while Elliott works 'from the inside out', Morris engages with the theatricality of the storytelling techniques that Stafford uses. His stated aim for the workshop is to "find whatever's live that tells the story" – and to make sure we're using the most vital means available to enrich each moment.

Morris tries to keep the room as open as possible to alternative ways of seeing, and staging, the scene. The actors read Stafford's scene first and discuss the psychology and motivations for their behaviour. The overlap of Morris and Elliott's techniques means that inspection of a scene as it reads on the page is followed by an improvisation of the action of that scene. Elliott will often summarise the scene in bullet-point format, giving key focus points for the actors to help them navigate the improvisation. Morris and Stafford supply historical perspective and information, and the actors begin to replay the scenes, allowing it to progress with variations.

Tim Lewis with Topthorn
(photograph by Simon Annand [SA])

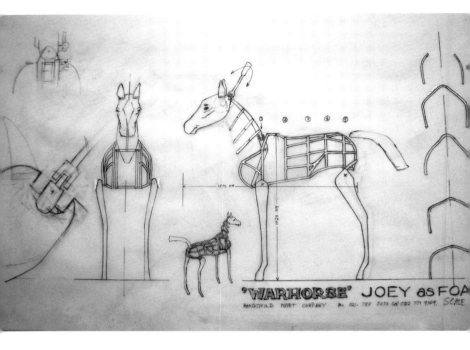

Adrian Kohler's technical drawings for Joey as a foal and the fully-grown Joey

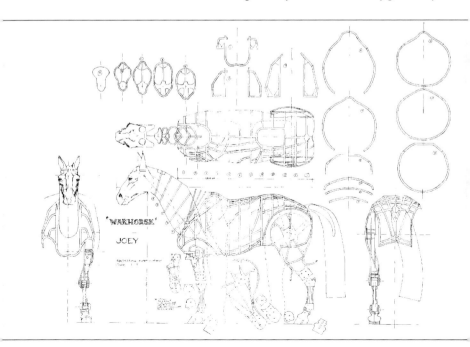

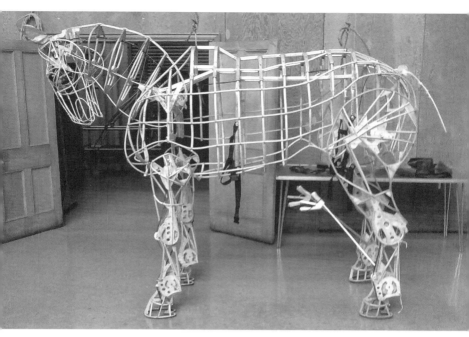

above: The prototype Joey for the 2006 workshop hanging in the NT Studio
(photograph by Mervyn Millar [MM])
below: Joey's mother (MM)

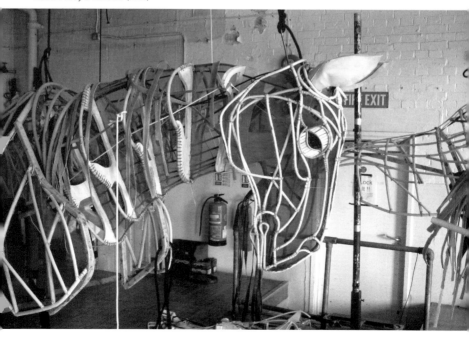

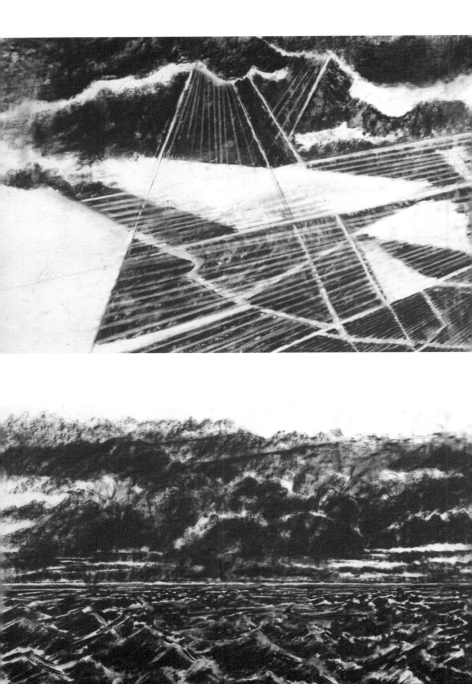

above and opposite: Drawings by Rae Smith for use on the screen

Emilie without hair or toes
(MM)

Allan Edwards and Basil Jones with rider puppets
(SA)

above: Emily Mytton with a crow (SA)
below: Rachel Leonard (in mustering horse) and Stephen Harper (MM)

above: Alice Barclay and Mervyn Millar with Emilie (photograph by Toby Olié)
below: Topthorn and Joey (SA)

Finn Caldwell with Goose
(SA)

above: Jamie Ballard with Joey (MM)
below: Angus Wright (SA)

above: Basil Jones and Adrian Kohler (SA)
below: Toby Sedgwick, Marianne Elliott and Vicki Liles (MM)

above: Nick Stafford (SA)
below: Toby Sedgwick, Tom Morris, Adrian Kohler and Basil Jones (SA)

above: Tom Morris, Michael Morpurgo and John Tams (MM)
below: Tom Morris, Nick Stafford, Paul Chequer, Finn Caldwell
and Toby Sedgwick playing Bally (MM)

above: Emily Mytton, Alice Barclay, Emilie, Rachel Leonard and Mervyn Millar (SA)
below: The War Horse company (SA)

Toby Sedgwick rehearses the death of Topthorn, with Tim Lewis and Craig Leo visible
(SA)

Sometimes the result pulls away from the shape that Stafford has laid out – but the inquiring spirit and the concise summary enable the actors to take strong choices with clear desires, and their instincts uncover new possibilities. So it's shocking in one improvisation when Ted, humiliated in front of the village at the auction, lashes out with his whip at Albert and sends him home, leaving him to struggle with the foal alone. We'd always played the scene with Albert present at its end – but this discovery energises the scene, and the relationship between the characters – it completes Ted's humiliation. So the team decide to rebuild the scene with this in it. Next, Stafford will take the ideas home, apply his economy of expression, and present the next version.

The process puts Stafford's work under close scrutiny before he might feel ready, and it can sometimes feel as if his work and his ability are being attacked or undermined. "All the things you would normally do in private, with one or two other people, are done in public," he explains:

It's very, very destabilising. If you can avoid feeling you're being personally attacked in public, remember that the concern is the work, and what will eventually appear on stage... if you can go home with that, that's fine. And sometimes I feel like I have managed it. There've been a couple of times when I've thought... 'I really could just walk out of here.' But then you think: but why? Walk out of what?

In the centre of the workshop, with a room full of people testing out their own ideas on top of his own, it's easy for Stafford to feel overwhelmed. But on a day like the one when actors and puppeteers alike get into horse puppets, raise up the figures of the riders on their backs and set up for the cavalry charge, it's clear that the sole focus of the directors and their team is to make the most extraordinary things happen on stage. Toby Sedgwick, given free rein to choreograph a possible finale of the disastrous charge, is full of vivid moving imagery, and as the actors and I step in to supplement the puppeteers, he has us attempting to simulate astonishing carnage in slow motion: horses tumbling tail over neck, riders slipping from their backs and falling beneath them, mounts sliding and crashing into one another. Like Morris, he's no respecter of what his personnel think they can do: he just asks them to do what he's imagining, and in most cases, they manage it.

Each workshop uses a different cast of actors, and within a workshop, roles are rotated between different actors, so the team are able to see a range of responses to the characters in these improvisations, and it's to the benefit of the *War Horse* script that over various workshops, different actors improvise the scenes. So Ted Narracott's character benefits from variations like Sedgwick's lugubrious drunk, Jim Bywater's exasperated, knot-faced incompetent, and Alan Williams' dry brute, and when Sedgwick will come to assemble the fuller character in rehearsals, he has plenty to draw on. The improvisations teach the directors a little more about what they might ask from Nick Stafford as the rewrites continue, and all three of them about how to make each character's journey through the story most satisfying. They hand the initiative back to Stafford as he goes back to rewrite – and as the further drafts come, sometimes we see scenes clearly inspired by what's happened in the improvisations, sometimes very different in response to them.

Joey's character needs to develop this way too. Tom Morris stresses that "We must remember always to think of the horse's objective," to ensure that it's at the centre of how the scene can be read by the audience. Adrian Kohler adds that the horse's objectives are often interrupted by the story's action – like so many heroes, he's almost never in control of the situation; and as Elliott notes early in the March 2006 workshop, another of our challenges is to find out what other characters need from the horse. What does Albert need to see to inspire his devotion to Joey? Morpurgo's characters often comment on Joey's fiery spirit – and as the puppeteers begin to master the controls of the puppet, they are also invited to bring emotion to the scenes they improvise. As always, Elliott's eye is on the subtext: "The horse represents to Ted everything he can't control about Albert," she observes after a particularly heated interaction. So Joey's character develops from Morpurgo's hints, the other characters' needs, and his own simple objectives – nearness to Albert, food, rest.

Workshopping is a rich way of generating and developing material for a script, but it's nothing without the gaps between the workshops. Nick Stafford and Adrian Kohler need to take away what they've learnt and apply themselves to their work, rewriting and replanning the shapes and details of the script and puppets respectively. Moments or ideas that seemed ingenious and perfect in the heady community of the workshop room can limp when examined more closely. And it takes time and thought to make the strong choices for the story structure, with the team conscious that, as Nick Hytner warns, "no amount of brilliant visual and physical work will cover up for a slack narrative, or a narrative that isn't emotionally involving." The working of the scene with actors reveals to Kohler what the demands on his puppet will be – so he needs to make sure the horse will be able to play the scene.

The Studio time is also about research, and the group, especially the puppeteers and directors, make visits to widen their experience of horses. The Working Horse Trust is a working farm in Kent that demonstrates to visitors the old ways of farming with horses. It's a great help to our understanding of how a horse works on a farm, and the team are happy to spend hours watching the horses, observing how a plough is hooked up and pulled, and hearing anecdotes about horses that have been there.

A couple of days later we are able to visit the King's Troop in their barracks in St John's Wood. The King's Troop are a mounted artillery regiment that still train using systems in place since before the First World War: they can be seen in action on state occasions, at tournaments and at displays, and practising every Tuesday and Friday morning on Wormwood Scrubs in London. It's an early start to meet Group Captain Mark Edwards, and several of the company have had to reach to the back of their wardrobes to comply with the 'no jeans' rule. But this visit is well worth it – as in the book, most of the regiment's horses are thoroughbred/Irish Draught crosses (like Joey), and the contrast between these well-trained mounts and the burly, opinionated characters at the farm is marked. Our host at the farm offered us plenty of material for the stoicism of the farmer living through bad times, and the characters here are equally obliging. Captain Edwards is a perfect gentleman, bright and cheery, with two beautifully-kept Labradors accompanying him. He's a diplomatic and informal conversationalist who one feels could have stepped straight out of an officer's mess of 1914. Sergeant-Major Gascoigne creates the sort of contrast that one might only expect in a well-planned fiction. He's a career soldier to whom the regiment is everything. He's keen to impress on us its history, honour and achievements, and is alarmingly ready to demonstrate the traditional weaponry skills – from running through an enemy whilst on horseback without getting dragged off one's mount, to tent-pegging (a display of accuracy in which a soldier on a galloping horse picks a tent-peg out of the ground with his lance). He's loud, confident, and direct throughout our chats with him, whereas Captain Edwards seems almost hesitant when talking to us (even though he's authoritative with his men). We watch impressive displays as the horses, six to a gun, practise their manoeuvres out on the Scrubs. Later, back at the barracks, we spend time seeing how the horses are groomed and kept in stable. The gunners we meet are brisk and deferential. Nick Stafford has a military background himself – his father and brother were both soldiers. Marianne Elliott is thoughtful and observant, allowing Toby Sedgwick's naturally gregarious character to put him forward as our spokesperson. Basil Jones and Adrian Kohler drink in all the detail, quietly photographing and filming.

Both here and at the farm, several of the company have been at pains to make sure we ask about the other side of horse-keeping – what happens when they die? We're painfully aware that we need to stage scenes in which men lose horses they love, horses lose men they have become attached to, and horses lose other horses. Neither farmer nor soldier seem prone to romanticise or anthropomorphise the emotions of the horses, although both have stories about how the surviving horses' behaviour changed when their companions were lost. For us, drawn to love stories, it's natural and easy to turn our horse into a romantic hero; but these people, who are around horses continuously for years, understand that the horse has its own standards of attachment which don't approximate human relationships.

· · ·

"In London everyone is working at the top of their game," thinks Cape Town-based Basil Jones. "You feel that people are just that much more fantastic, that much more engaged, that much more hardworking and enthusiastic than in other places. Because there's a lot of competition here. And that's wonderful, particularly when you've got 14 people in a room, all specialising in a different aspect of theatre, so you're seeing 14 really superb practitioners. And there's a remarkable lack of ego, I think, in everybody, which enables 14 people to work together: otherwise it would be impossible." As the workshops have continued, Morris and Elliott's team has expanded. Rae Smith is a key addition, but also crucial to their planning are the technical artists who did so much to make *Coram Boy* a stunning experience in the theatre: lighting designer Paule Constable and sound designer Christopher Shutt. Other new faces are video designers FiftyNine – Leo Warner and his colleague Mark Grimmer. The Studio time is limited, and each of the creatives is busy – so it can be a struggle to get everyone in the right place at the right time to try everything that they want to see.

Designer Rae Smith is present throughout the third, 2007 workshop, observing and building up tools for her planning. Another key stage of the Studio-based development process was a week in November 2006 when Smith and Handspring spent an intensive week together, making connections between their visual worlds to lay out the possible languages for the show. One of Smith's key tools is the set model, and she and assistant Will Fricker present various objects made at 1:25 scale to plot through scenes before trying them with the company. And she also begins to build two other key documents. One is a full storyboard that will become our main guide to the production. It includes, for each scene, a sketch of the stage space, an idea of what happens during the scene, who's involved, and what the sound and lighting effects might be. In terms of developing the overall visual sequence of the show, it's essential, and it continues to develop right up to rehearsals. She is also beginning to plot a chart of which actor will play which character when. This will get developed with the directors and, while it'll certainly be useful for casting purposes later, Smith needs to have some idea of how many times actors will be changing costumes to get a sense of how the piece can look. She has plenty to keep her busy, but the rest of the team are keen for her to be in the room contributing. She herself sees her work as collaborative:

Essentially, I will spend the whole time in the workshop just watching, and suggesting, and looking at things and telling you whether it's clear or unclear. Whether it seems to be an interesting idea or a crap idea. And what's really good about something rather than what's really bad about it. I think if you talk with a whole group of people about what's good or interesting or clear about something, then the group's mind can define it. People who are cleverer or have a deeper understanding of a particular aspect of that something can solve the problem, or the thing that's unclear to you.

The *War Horse* workshop room is a fecund place for imagination, and a surprisingly generous one. Ideas come and go – for a long period there was definitely going to be a puppet dog that accompanied the puppet Emilie through a field of poppies. For a while it was everyone's favourite character in the piece. But as things moved on, it became clear that there wasn't a place for that scene in the flow of the story. When the challenge is posed as to how we show the crucial moment of the horses and men crossing the channel, there are ideas from all quarters. Basil Jones suggests a sea of human hands, passing and manipulating puppet boats. Tom Morris' mind's eye has a 'close-up' scene focusing on a deck, contrasting the effects of sea travel on men and horses; Rae Smith is thinking about the Olivier's drum revolve rising to isolate horses on the deck, with the men visible, cabined below. Adrian Kohler offers a movement sequence of small boats manipulated across the stage, and video artist Mark Grimmer suggests the same 'long shot' seen on screen, with shadow puppets or animation. Any of these, alone or in combination, would be enough to hold and deliver the sequence. Although the idea that we go into rehearsals with is none of these, but another of Smith's – to take that staple of low-budget theatre, the sea of billowing fabric, and expand it across the vastness of the Olivier's round stage.

The room is always full of ideas and suggestions, and yet when Marianne Elliott looks back on the workshops, one of her strongest memories is of a sequence, just after this one, which seemed utterly daunting.

> When Joey gets off the boat in France, and we thought, 'Oh God, how's that going to work, how's that going to work?' – do you remember? They see wounded English soldiers passing, and Nicholls does a salute and puts Joey in the way, and you're not quite sure if Joey is protecting Nicholls, or Nicholls has put him in the way so that people can't see his emotion.
>
> And I thought, 'That is not going to work. That is clearly not going to work, how are we going to do that?' Do you remember those long discussions we had, 'How shall we do it? Shall we have big faces on the screen, wounded faces, blood pouring?' – and where are they going to travel to?
>
> But then, we did it in the workshop and it was just so simple.

One other sequence that receives plenty of attention is a key storytelling moment that can't be handled by the traditional scriptwriting process. The early scenes require a young foal, vulnerable and lively, to be contrasted with his larger mother. But by the time Joey is asked to plough a field, he is fully grown – and the audience need to understand that the new puppet is the same character as the old one: a handover must take place. A moment like this, or the almost dialogue-free scene in which the puppet child Emilie meets Joey, has to be told visually, with any scripted speech responding to a shape that's determined by staging and developed through the puppeteers and actors improvising and responding to direction.

There are other routes for material and relationships to surface, especially as we approach elements of the story that are peripheral to Joey's direct perspective. Michael Morpurgo offers a sad and beautiful moment in which Trooper Warren (in our version the son of Ted Narracott's rival, tormentor and brother-in-law) shelters, shell-shocked, in the military stables at the Front, taking solace from the bulk and breath of the calm Joey and Topthorn. The scene is as much about the frame of mind that shell-shock induces as it is about the individual experience of Warren or Joey. And it's difficult to improvise from a standing start.

Tom Morris, especially, is interested in how people and animals communicate without speaking – certainly a new subject to explore in the theatre. His way is to lead an exercise in which one actor plays a soldier and all of the others play 'the war', with the ability to surprise him with memories and hallucinations of explosions. It doesn't take long to bully Stephen Harper (improvising Warren) into a terror, and when Joey is released into the room, a winning image emerges: Ned Warren crawling into a very dangerous place – between the horse's hooves – to take refuge from his imaginary bombardment. *War Horse*'s story is built from the foundations of Morpurgo's narrative via moments like these. One of the strengths of the *War Horse* development is that some scenes arrive from this physical direction, others through Stafford's careful writing – and never in competition. Each language expands or steps aside to accommodate the other. Nick Stafford talks about the collaboration being the creation of a "story that we collectively are nudging each other towards." There's no existing template for working out how to make a script like this, as Stafford reflects:

Sometimes people talk about their process, and I often think: I don't know what this 'process' is. You know, it doesn't exist, apart from us. We are the process. Tom sets things up, and Marianne, and Basil and Adrian set things up – they build Joey the way they build it, and it provokes certain responses in people. So there's always one thing leading to another…

And Elliott is clear about why the workshop proceeds so smoothly. She could be talking about any of her collaborators when she discusses her relationship with Handspring: "They're brilliant. Because they're very open, and they're creative in terms of the whole piece. So we're all putting ideas together, about the writing, about things that may not be anything to do with puppets. About the design, about the story… and they're able to do that in a non-threatening way, I suppose you've got to be quite generous of spirit. It's always felt like a team."

Rae Smith reflects a similar feeling about how the show will come across to the audience:

I think the relationships between all the different disciplines have more of a chance of living seamlessly together, as if it were a part of one world and one imagination, called the story, because we've spent time together – not so much talking about what we do, but seeing what the other does. It's the opposite to war, and I think, like any art project, theatre does that: it builds things which you can't talk about, as opposed to destroying things that you can't talk about. It's particularly true of theatre, because it's so much about making something together and then looking at it, talking about it, and doing it again.

Purni Morell observes that "we at the Studio don't define the relationship we have with people or projects: they do. It's one of the really nice things about the Studio actually, that it has this momentary but complete involvement in something or someone's life. So, a project will kind of do what it does, will come here for three weeks, and then go away and we'll never see it again… It's a very momentary but quite intense relationship."

Making all of these workshops possible, working alongside the Studio's own small but dedicated team, are the National Theatre's production management and stage management staff. *War Horse* is allocated experienced personnel: Sacha Milroy as production manager and Jane Suffling as stage manager. Jane has worked at the NT for 25 years, and knows everything about its workings. She's full of enthusiasm about the project, and her energy communicates through her team, Ian Connop, Vicki Liles and Cynthia Duberry, who support us. One of Suffling's great assets is how ready she is for the next eventuality, and how supportive she is of new ideas. When someone suggests that Ted Narracott might try using a whip to intimidate young Joey, she's ready to arrange a training session in whip-cracking; when we're considering using farm equipment as limbs and structures for our experiments in simulating horse-movement, we arrive the next day to find not only a barnful of hoes and barrows, but also some built-up hoof-shoes from the original production of *Equus*, all sourced promptly from the NT's stores.

Nicholas Hytner tells me that he likes to step back from his colleagues' creative processes. "I want them to run in the most unexpected and the most creative directions," he says. The Studio time has been all about creativity. His role is as the head of the producing theatre and his focus is on the final production. He's available to Morris, Elliott and Stafford as they produce drafts of the script, to lend his comments on the storytelling. "It's best to be quite ruthless and demanding in asking those who are writing and directing to address fully what it is they're trying to do and whether they really think they've achieved it yet," he says. Hytner, as an encouraging yet critical ear for the script development, is part of the machinery of production at the National.

Production manager Sacha Milroy is at work on *War Horse* much earlier than she might otherwise be. "Normally you miss out the very early creative stage," she says. "I don't think there's been another project, especially at the National, where a production manager's been involved so early on in the process." The reason is, as Nick Stafford notes, "something unique about this process: that from the very start, the main concern is what appears on stage." As the workshops have continued, there's been a sense that all of the collaborators are focused on the achievable show – and are circling in on a common vision. And because they want to know what's possible as well as what would might be desirable, they need Milroy to help work it out.

It's her job to supervise all the technical and practical aspects of the show – to make sure that the great ideas happening in the rehearsal room are able to make it onto the Olivier stage. Along the way, she's been making sure we have what we need for the workshops. Each room that we've worked in has required scaffolding for the horses to be hung on; and tools brought across so that Adrian Kohler and Allan Edwards (on attachment from the NT's props department and invaluable in making design adjustments to the puppets), can work on maintaining and improving the horses. They do this work early in the mornings, through lunchtimes, and into the evenings so as not to disrupt the day's exploration.

Both workshops required a week in a dark space so that Mark Grimmer and Leo Warner could offer their video techniques. In 2006, we moved from the Studio to one of the main rehearsal rooms at the NT. In 2007, Sacha's team transport all the horses and equipment from the Studio's temporary home in Kennington to the backstage space in the Lyttelton, usually used for storing the sets of shows that are in rep. We work there even when matinees are in progress only yards away.

A few weeks after the final workshop, Milroy explains how the next phase of her job will work:

We get an allocation of budget, and then an allocation of hours: so many carpentry hours, so many paintframe hours, and propmaking hours, and armoury. Then, anything you use over that, you have to convert into cash. I have to work out a schedule of building, and for this production, we need to start building a little earlier, because we have to get some of the scenery into the rehearsal room. So it's a build schedule through to a technical schedule, for when we get into the theatre. I have to work out the order of events, how we rig the scenery, who has which slot, when the technical rehearsals start, the dress rehearsal, and co-ordinate the creative team about what they'd like and when they'd like it – while keeping it all in budget.

And Rae Smith explains what is different about the production process for *War Horse*. "Sometimes, in theatre, you design something and it eventually turns up on stage, but in this case, we build it and put it in the rehearsal room, because we need to make sure it works." Smith is embracing the puppetry language of the show, and instead of solid, permanent scenic elements, she imagines objects that take their place when they are needed, and are manipulated and enfolded into the scene. "Everything that we are going to use as part of the performance goes through the rehearsal room first."

Rae knows from her previous work that "at the National Theatre, they know the heart of the matter is in the process of making work. They have production departments that support that, which means we can have these workshops – that have allowed us not just to come together conceptually, but also in

45

terms of how we do things." Smith and the creative team need to work closely with Milroy to guide them as to what they can achieve or attempt. Milroy says 'no' much less often than you might expect, given the imaginative leaps the creative process can make. But Smith is conscious of the demands that she's making. "The whole process of trying things out in rehearsal means that you have to go to the production manager, and instead of saying, 'this is the design', giving them the framework in which we are now going to proceed: a blueprint in which the physical realisation of the show can occur."

Smith's confidence in Sacha Milroy is well placed. But the NT needs to stretch to accommodate this unique show. "We don't have a puppet workshop," explains Milroy. "When we did the last production with puppets, *His Dark Materials*, we ended up having to bring people in from outside and set up our own completely different department." In this case, Allan Edwards, who has been involved from the first workshops, provides a link to the NT's props-making department, and Adrian Kohler and Basil Jones's work on the puppets fits in at the NT much more smoothly.

Tom Morris is put on the back foot when I ask him at what point the show was definitely going to be programmed. He thinks back uncertatinly before hazarding that "after last June's workshop it was definitely going to happen". One of the reasons he's unsure is because "we didn't do a showing… but people popped in and had a look… and got excited enough about, well, the horse, basically. Which is bizarre. It's horse-based programming."

3. **The Horses**

It's a whole other world. It's like… stepping on Mars for a bit.

Marianne Elliott

"THE KIND OF WORK I know about from BAC," says Tom Morris, "a lot of it goes into rehearsal without knowing what it is, and it is therefore effectively made in a rehearsal room. This play is a hybrid between that sort of BAC-style devised show and some gargantuan Hollywood film where, almost, you know what the 'product' is – in this case, it's a horse. Everything else is evolving to support that. We're a strange hybrid of a 'fringey' devised process and a kind of no-prisoners-will-be-taken, high-production-values, movie-style process."

Since the day Adrian Kohler and Basil Jones revealed their full-size prototype puppet horse, a new spring and confidence has attended the development of *War Horse*. Whenever a scene seems awkward, discussed around the table, a glance across the room at the hanging horse puppets offers a reminder that words aren't the only currency of this production – and an attempt to look at a scene with the horse in it transforms it completely.

Handspring have been making extraordinary puppets for 25 years, but only ten years ago, puppetry was still largely seen as a medium for children. Sophisticated and surprising uses of puppetry went unnoticed in children's shows, or were restricted to a small circuit of artistic productions seen by small audiences. But that has changed. Puppetry has become more common in large shows in London and across the world's big stages. Basil Jones of Handspring isn't worried that the use of puppetry on a large scale will faze a London audience. "Most theatre audiences will have seen quite wonderful puppets in recent times on stage; there's an amazing wealth of expertise," he says. Citing productions including Disney's *The Lion King* and the National Theatre's *His Dark Materials*, he goes on: "Puppetry has become part of the theatre vocabulary that is used by everyone, including all the top directors that you'd like to name – they've all used puppets in the last 20 years." His partner Adrian Kohler concurs, asserting that he never considers that the use of puppets might be difficult for an audience. What he strives for, he says, is to find something original to do with his puppetry. In *War Horse*, however, because an animal puppet is the story's central character, and goes on a genuine emotional journey as the main audience focus: "I really do feel it will be a new puppet experience."

Kohler and Jones have given most of the past two years to making *War Horse.* The British funding system doesn't often allow for venues to book them in this country, and you can see that they sense it's an opportunity to do something very special for an audience that doesn't know their work that well. "In a movie," says Kohler, "it would be a real horse performing the role – and ultimately there would always be that human-horse barrier, because, you know a horse cannot play a part in the way a human can. In this piece, the horse can do exactly what he wants to do, and from what I've seen in the workshop, if we can shape that into what it promises to be, it can be incredibly strong, incredibly emotional." The judgment and timing of the puppeteer as an actor is critical to the characterisation of Joey – his temper, his vigour and spirit. The central challenge for Kohler as a puppet designer has been to provide a mechanical system that allows three puppeteers working together to create that animal behaviour convincingly.

Kohler knows how to make puppets – and yet with every design there is a step into the unknown, a new test of his ability, and an uncertainty about whether it will work. He's always ready to adapt and improve the design where he can. Handspring's work has seen puppets and people working together on stage many, many times before, and yet, here it seems a little different. Perhaps it's because in this story, the first puppets seen are animals, and it's so long before you see a puppet human interact with an actor. Perhaps it's because the story that the group are telling hinges so centrally on a simple relationship between the animal and the boy. And perhaps it's because this horse is the subtlest and most intricate of his designs to date – the most naturalistic. "They walk on the same ground as the people, they're about the right size for a horse, and they can do quite a lot of horse movements convincingly, so, you quickly get over the… puppet thing, the *puppetness* of them," he says. "What's excited me most is the amount of language that these horse puppets seem to be able to embody, and the way in which people and horses can seem to interact very well on this stage. The distinction between puppets and people doesn't seem so great, for some reason."

There was a good deal of nervousness, as Kohler recalls, when they brought the first prototype to London in June 2006. The shipping from Cape Town set him an unavoidable deadline and, as always, he ended up working till the last minute.

We built the prototype, booked a place on the ship, and built a crate for it. I was hoping to walk it about Kalk Bay as a test before I packed it up, but, as always happens, it was only finished the night before it left. And so we walked it around, and took some still pictures, as if it was galloping… and emailed those off to London. But I was extremely nervous as to whether it would really perform.

If he was nervous putting the puppet in the crate, he was more so taking it out. In a rehearsal room in the NT Studio on The Cut, we'd assembled a company of British actors and puppeteers, along with an expectant Marianne Elliott and Nick Stafford, to take part in the next phase of the workshop process.

> *We had a whole lot of people come in on the first day of that workshop, and I was kind of terrified to meet them and the puppet in the same day, but it soon became clear that the figure was going to work.*

Basil Jones continues:

> *Adrian has designed the horses so beautifully that they're actually very easy to manipulate, easier than I thought. They moved magnificently right from the start: when someone gets in and starts operating it, within an hour it's working pretty well. I thought it was going to take a lot longer.*

Elliott declares: "It's magical. When you make them alive, they're really *there*. And it's even more magical than that: you can see the manipulators, and yet, that animal, that character is really *there*." She has no prior experience of working with puppetry and is a terrific judge of what works on stage – so her responses were amongst the most keenly awaited by the puppet design team. And as the horses developed, Elliott was increasingly won over. She remembers seeing the final Joey and Topthorn puppets at the 2007 workshop:

> *When we saw the horses, and they were so much more articulated than they had been last time, they started to look like these beings – these big, beastly beings. That was really eye-opening, realising what a puppet could do, I suppose, and the skill in making those puppets.*

Nick Stafford, typically, finds a telling detail to communicate his sense of wonder at the intricacy, experience and artistry at work in the construction of the puppets: "I think: what a fantastic piece of machinery this is. Then I look down, and holding the joint in Joey's leg together is an elastic band. A little, tiny elastic band like the postman chucks on the ground outside my house."

• • •

Kohler's design process starts with a pencil and paper, and some rough, dynamic drawings:

> I like life-drawing, I like working from the actual form, and then seeing how much of that I need. I work from the skeletons of animals. If you work on the bone proportions of an animal and you string that all together, it automatically gives you the movement of the creature you are building, and that goes a long way to convincing an audience. Movement is paramount. I trust that.

Handspring made a series of shows with the acclaimed South African artist William Kentridge, with whom they worked closely. Kohler remembers Kentridge's contribution to the style. "He always said 'Draw from the shoulder, not from the elbow or the wrist' – and that does give you a stronger line, and, when I'm carving, the freedom to gouge a face out." The freedom of line in his drawings and the faithfulness to the real skeleton in his designs, are, he says, his key principles.

Kohler's next task is to work out how the figure will be manipulated. A puppet the size of a horse, intended to interact freely with actors, will certainly need more than one manipulator. And each moving part of the puppet will need to be under the control of someone's hand. Kohler's observation of horses, and his experience with his giant giraffe puppet from 2004, indicates that the ears and tail will be key expressive features. The story requires Joey and Topthorn to be ridden, another structural demand. Kohler's design sketches include manipulators, a way of puzzling out how they fit into the picture:

> *Quite a lot of those early pictures had people manipulating the horse from outside. Clearly, if they were to be ridden, they had to be supported from inside, so that was a given, but I didn't really know how the head was going to work, and I was proposing all sorts of lifts, external manipulators lifting the horse so it could rear up and stuff.*

Handspring's puppets have always been visibly manipulated. Their human puppets are usually designed without legs and carried by manipulators to occupy a space slightly above and beside the other actors. Their giraffe was operated by two people on stilts, using their own legs for the giraffe's. One, in the rear, operated the tail and ears, and the other, in front, the head and neck. This time it is more critical that the horse's leg movements are convincing. Previous puppets they have built, which have had 'realistic' legs, have been too small for people to be inside, with the legs operated from beside the puppet. But that system won't work for these horses.

The other concern is what the puppet will look like. Do we want puppet horses that look like real horses in texture and colour? Handspring's tradition has always been to leave their wooden figures unpainted and with mechanisms partly visible to the audience – there's no pretence that these are anything other than puppets. Kohler needs to start from another, more practical principle and then negotiate the consequences for how the puppet might look. "I felt all along that I would build the puppet from the inside out, from what it needed, structurally.

And then step back and say, what does it actually look like, can we bear the aesthetic it's proposing?"

The two tyrants of puppet design are strength and weight. They're frequently in opposition. The need for strength pulls the design in one direction, but a heavy puppet is awkward and difficult to manipulate – and lightweight materials are rarely the strongest.

The first horses we develop in the workshops are actually not puppets at all. But Kohler and Jones build on the 'unadorned human horses' that emerge in workshops led by Tom Morris and Toby Sedgwick, adding quickly-made cardboard horse heads and manes to the image. To test how a rider might be held, a stout wooden ladder is made and suspended between two pairs of shoulders – with the rider between them. Even later, in workshops after the horse prototype has been developed, we still refer back to the simplest ways of representing a horse, adding in separate horse-puppet legs or heads to create partial horse images. Kohler is used to making partial puppets, and Morris' invitation is always to "think about what it does, rather than what it looks like." Marianne Elliott endorses this approach, and not just for the workshops but also through to the final performance: "We have to tell the audience right up front that they're going to use their imagination with what they see."

Kohler and Jones are often hands-on in these situations, taking the place of puppeteers and adding their sensitivity and experience to the scenes. These experiments with partial horses form part of our aesthetic throughout. It's clear that not every horse in the story can be represented in full, especially if three manipulators are needed, and it's incumbent on the designers to identify which parts of the horse image contribute most to the characterisation of the individual horse, and also to the larger image of a group of horses on stage.

The bodies of Kohler's puppets in the past have usually been made from plywood sections. But for the fluid lines of the horse bodies, he decided to take another route: cane. "Cane is a much more flexible medium; it's very light, and it also can take quite a lot of bending and pushing about when in the actual figure," he says. A key participant in this decision was Kohler's new assistant maker in Cape Town, Thys Stander.

Stander, remembers Kohler, developed a way of shaping the cane very precisely, sewing it to a set of plywood shapes, some of which were removed once the cane had dried into the desired shape. The result was a "combination of layers of cane frame that are linked with dowels through the plywood sections, which makes quite a rigid box, basically, with flexible elements." The flexibility is critical to the puppets, which are bound to take some knocks in rehearsal and performance. Cane has a natural spring in it that gives these puppet bodies a tolerance for accident that a more brittle material might not offer. And seen in three dimensions, the cane is an improvement on the plywood in terms of line, too, as Kohler observes. "Plywood can be sinuous in one dimension but it's absolutely straight in the other. Cane can form a sinuous three-dimensional structure."

So with cane asserting itself as the most practical basic material for the horses' structure, the question became: could the creative team bear puppets made with a cane framework? One missing feature is the flesh, the meat, the muscle of a real horse. Another, observed Marianne Elliott, was the softness of an animal's coat and hair – something that would become crucial to the design of the mane and tail to allow them to move well. Basil Jones is concerned by the sound the puppets make. The horses' mechanisms make a noise of their own, and initially the hooves clatter and slip on the rehearsal room floor (we eventually 'shoe' them with thin gripping foam). In one workshop, we experiment, too, with what Tom Morris called a 'sound puppet' – a gym vaulting-horse at the edge of the playing area that could be slapped and patted to create the sound of hand on horsehide. The hard-working puppeteers inside the horses do a convincing job of conveying the strain and muscle of the animal in action. In any puppet, the movement must be more persuasive than the form. With the increasing skill of the puppeteers in showing a detailed, breathing, connected figure, the rigid lines of cane seem sometimes to ripple and shift in breath and strain.

For the final Joey and Topthorn, Kohler developed the simple cane grid of the prototype into a more individual and flowing line emphasising the animal's anatomy. There are technical adjustments to allow the head operator to switch sides and operate the ears, and the horse's head to reach the ground. The horses are made slightly larger than life-size to allow the internal manipulators to fit inside without their heads protruding. These developments, and other variations, are designed by Kohler, Thys Stander and Allan Edwards from seeing the horse tested in the workshop room.

The other horses are to be simpler versions of Joey and Topthorn. For Alice, Joey's mother, the designers imagine a symbol of motherhood. Even bigger than the other horses, they see her as tentlike, with a waterfall of tail hanging behind: a home that Joey wants to return to. As she does not need to be ridden, her spine can be made with a swivelling joint – which will give her a unique rolling movement.

At many stages in the workshop, especially without the full complement of puppets, horses have been pulled together out of the props of farming and war, using a well-established visual language in the theatre to transform objects into puppets. One of those times is when we approach the gun team. The horses pulling the gun carriage need to look half-dead; in the book there are four, but even the Olivier stage can't fit a six-horse gun team on it – so we have only Coco and Heine, characters we begin to refer to as the Horses of Death. These exhausted horses are to be further variations on the Joey and Topthorn design. In workshop, broken wood and tools are used to give these horses a transient, fragile form, but Kohler wants to offer vivid, poetic, sculptural animals, and Jones is concerned about the metaphorical suggestion that the animals are built up out of human tools, or are mechanical beings. Kohler's final designs for Coco and Heine are twisted, flayed, half-functioning, travesties of the smoothly-working Joey and Topthorn puppets.

The Younger Joey puppet is just as difficult. Clearly he will be too small for the puppeteers to get inside. We attempt part-human, part-puppet figures. We try the simplest image of a horse that we can make – just a head, and then a tail to join it. Someone grabs some short lengths of two-by-one timber to use as skinny, straight legs, and it's one of the great serendipitous moments of the development. The kneeless legs make the foal's walking elongated, clumsy, fragile and awkward. Next to Alice – the idea of a horse, with no visible legs but only a long skirt to the ground – this smaller figure looks vulnerable, naïve and helpless. There are three puppeteers hunched over this partial image, but its expressive movement is strong enough to let them shift into the background. Kohler adds a quickly-made shape of bamboo for a body and we have the beginning of the foal puppet. As with Coco and Heine, Kohler takes this rough mock-up as inspiration to create a more shaped, structured puppet for the rehearsal period.

As a sculptor, Kohler is acutely conscious of how 'realistic' or not his puppets are – they are much more faithful to the shape of a real horse than many other puppet designers' might be. "There is a naturalistic element," he confirms, "plus an element of expressionism as well, in the lines you're using in making the figure." The cane lines of the *War Horse* horses are emphasised by the decision to put their 'skin' inside their structure rather than stretching it over the outside as with previous Handspring designs.

Handspring use thin, stretchy, coloured polyester georgette – which becomes partly transparent under theatre lights. The puppeteers inside are visible, but not distractingly so. The lines of the cane are unified and joined together; the edges of the figure become more defined. And keeping the beauty of the cane lines on the outside of the puppet asserts their status as sculptural objects – these are beautiful because of the marriage of function and sculpture in their design, not in spite of it. *War Horse* invites the audience to participate in a type of imaginative game; part of it is to accept these horses as they are.

• • •

No-one knows how to manipulate these horses. Adrian Kohler has developed the mechanisms based on previous systems, but the puppeteers in the workshops develop their own intuitive relationships with the systems, while those of us on the outside are able to take in the picture of what they are trying and offer suggestions.

Even though, as Basil Jones noted, the puppets move pretty well straight away, there's plenty to do to get really precise and convincing movement. But the directors are an enthusiastic initial audience. Even within a couple of days, Tom Morris is marvelling at the progress: "it's a breakthrough every five minutes," he beams as the puppeteers go into a real-time trot. Some difficulties are based on pure strength and weight distribution – initially it's very difficult to walk persuasively when the puppet has a rider on it – but as the rehearsals continue, the puppeteers literally grow into their roles, and with plenty of drilling, this problem, like so many others, disappears.

Kohler is and has always been a puppeteer himself and so when he designs and builds his puppets he is aware of what the puppeteer wants from the object. "The puppeteers need a figure that moves well," he says, "that gives them a range of possibilities, and a strong character to play." The puppet sculptor is the writer of the character, and the puppeteer's first act is to begin interpreting that character. Handspring are a practical company, too, who are used to making, working and fixing their own puppets. There's little pretension about how they do their work or how they treat their figures, which are relatively robust. In some traditions or cultures, the puppet itself is treated as something that carries a mystical or semi-religious charge; but these are theatre-makers who happen to have taken the design of their figures to new heights. When we find that we will have actors picking up and carrying 'dead' puppets on stage, and the question arises as to whether they are treated with reverence or ceremony, the answer is clear. The puppets are tools for performance and the puppeteers are people who use those tools. They are treated with respect and with care, but not with artificial ritual. Just as the puppeteer, and the act of animation, is always visible to the audience, so here the difference between an animated and unanimated figure is exposed fully for the audience to observe – and when the horses are re-inhabited for the second cavalry action, the audience are able to see the transformation happen.

Kohler is honest enough to admit he is no expert on horses: "But fortunately Toby Sedgwick lives next to horses, and he came with a lot of information about their behaviour. Now, I'd looked at a lot of horses, but I'd been looking at them to see how I could make a flesh-and-bone head out of cane, I hadn't been looking at how they behaved."

Unleashed on the horse puppets, Sedgwick is irrepressible, a constant monologue of detail – as the puppeteers grasp one note, he is already moving on to the next one. The quality of movement develops by tiny discoveries to do with the angle of a hoof, or the precise weight exchange from leg to leg, and as he adds characteristic behavioural language, the puppets more and more become horses, and Tommy Luther and Toby Olié develop a better understanding as the inside of Joey. Both Sedgwick and Kohler are such enthusiasts that they would gladly spend days just perfecting these movements. Their attention to detail will be crucial when presenting convincing moments in the play – Joey jumping barbed wire, or the horse's kicks, for example, require hours of patient work to put the muscle movements in the right order.

The question of breath is a crucial one in puppetry, and it's necessary for the puppeteers to allow the horse's breath to be carried in their knees and in their shoulders. Kohler has designed a special feature in the horse's shoulders to allow these movements of the puppeteer's body to be visible. A lot of other work is focused on getting the sense of weight in the right place (into the hindquarters), and on making sure we always give the impression that the back legs push the horse off – when of course in fact the front puppeteer is leading the movement.

There's always more to do. As we plot through a 'conversation' between Albert and Joey in a workshop, after a scene between the family, making a note of all the moments that we need the audience to take note of, it's clear in comparison how easily we take in the unspoken behaviour between two actors. The physical language of the actor is beautifully, subtly expressive – and we need to teach the audience what a horse means when it turns away or flicks its tail. The fact that many of them will know plenty about real horses only means that it's more important that we get it as right as possible.

"We have to make their behaviour with one another convincing," says Adrian Kohler of the horses after the workshops are over. "We have to show the horse character going through trials, and we have to show the effects of those trials on the horse. At the moment we have only scratched the surface of that."

The results of these efforts will only become apparent in performance – long after I'm writing this. The workshops were useful for finding technical clues as to how we might convey things. During rehearsals we are spending time working towards the rhythms of Joey and Topthorn's thought, and the different characters of the horses just as we are developing the playing of the two-legged characters. It'll take much more than we displayed in the workshops to keep an audience's focus on the puppet throughout the show – both emotionally and technically. It's this combination that we hope we can achieve with Kohler and Jones' experience, the puppeteers' intuition and skill, and the directors' judgement and eye.

The journey towards plausible horse behaviour begins with research. One of the first things we watched in our first workshop was a video of the work of 'horse whisperer' Monty Roberts – who claims to speak 'equus', the physical language of horses. Books and anecdotes help us to compile an understanding of horse psychology and behaviour, and the roles of aggression and passivity in their relationships. The puppeteers become well-versed in tell-tale signs – a dropping head, a strong movement, squared legs. Experiences with real horses are exchanged, and the behaviour of the horses we visit at the farm, barracks and stables are analysed in detail. One recurrent theme is that the horses seem to take great pleasure in patiently and dryly making people who try to push them around look ridiculous. With our scene of Topthorn's death in our minds, we are also fascinated by stories about horses' behaviour when their stablemates die.

When we take a look at this scene in workshop it's instantly moving. One of the things puppets do best is die gracefully. Marianne Elliott is quick to spot that the key moment is when the manipulators leave the puppet. "It's like the soul leaving the body," she says. Basil Jones brings tradition and experience to the staging of this moment: "Whenever we have a puppet die this way," he says, "the movement away is like this." And his movement is beautiful: simple, understated, respectful.

As we enter rehearsal, the first thing to do (similar to the last workshop) is to sketch out the shape of the new draft over three weeks. It leaves little time for detailed puppet work, and the trios of manipulators can sometimes struggle to respond cohesively to actors thinking on their feet. The last hour of the day is always taken up with puppetry, allowing us to add a little finesse to what has been found during the day. And the puppeteers benefit from two weeks of training before rehearsals start. This time has allowed them to gain familiarity with the controls of the puppets and to establish the teams which will operate each figure – their precise casting, unlike the actors', has not been firmly determined. The training period is also the beginning of a programme of voice and fitness work. Working these heavy puppets over a long run puts serious strain on the puppeteers' bodies, and visits from physiotherapists help us to learn programmes of exercise to strengthen the right muscles and correct our bad habits. The puppeteers will also be making the sounds of the horses, and Kate Godfrey from the NT's voice department guides us through exercises to preserve and prepare our voices to whinny, whicker and neigh (and croak or honk in the case of the crows and goose).

Much more needs to be developed over the rehearsals. Character work on Joey and Topthorn is discussed with all the puppeteers, to find what role Joey's temper has on his relationships with humans and horses. It seems to be the key to a number of scenes but it can be difficult to keep in mind when playing the horse within a scripted framework. Even in workshops it was common to find Toby Sedgwick and Marianne Elliott calling from the sidelines: "You don't like the reins, Joey! Pull back, Joey! Getting angry, Albert!" Especially early in rehearsal, it's vital to keep the characters' responses honest even if it seems on the surface to play against the scene as written; the alternative is for the clash to arise later, when there is less time to acknowledge and build around it. Topthorn too has a distinctive character, and although many characters discuss him as a typical thoroughbred – fragile, temperamental, haughty – the story illustrates his other qualities – loyalty, and a determination that almost matches Joey's.

It's telling that the written script for Joey and Topthorn's meeting is minimal. In creative team meetings plotting through the show, too, there are few prescriptive proposals. Stafford and the rest of the team know that it needs to be developed from the characters of the horses. And the team understand, too, that this sequence, above all others, must be a clear puppetry moment, with as little support from the score or the screen as possible – an opportunity for the production to put forward what the puppets can do with movement, rhythm, mood and intention. Our researches indicate that dominant male horses can be pretty brutal to each other in establishing their hierarchy, and this supports the general desire to avoid sentimentalising the horse behaviour.

The puppetry has an effect on the creative team. The puppets become articles of faith for them, as Nick Stafford describes: "I don't understand puppets, in a way that I can talk about, but the effect is extraordinary. It's better than a live wire. Because it doesn't have to have any meaning… I don't know what sort of words to use about it which don't sound quasi-religious, but there's something like that going on."

Even when he hasn't seen the puppets themselves, Michael Morpurgo knows from talking to others the effect they have been having: "If, as I hope and believe, something extraordinary is going to come out of it, the puppetry is going to be at the centre of the extraordinariness," he says.

Another crucial aspect of Handspring's expertise is the shadow puppetry work in *War Horse*, allowing the personal story of Albert and Joey to expand to carry mythical, symbolic and epic content. In the past they have used a technique of visible puppetry with small, torn figures, being projected live onto a large screen; Rae Smith takes this idea and makes it the dominant visual motif of the production, with a glorious strip of torn paper arcing around the Olivier space above the action. It can be seen in different ways at different times, she explains: "It could be a cloud-line, but it could literally be a landscape. Or it could be a sky, or a seam of mist. It has a cyclorama aspect, and it contains the shadow work, and moving dynamics, and drawing. It will directly hold and focus what is going on in front of it." But "the magic of the storytelling," she says, "depends on the seamless blend" between the screen and stage action. It's a wonderful opportunity for Mark Grimmer and Leo Warner, of video design company FiftyNine. The availability of this cinematic perspective is a wonderful cue to all the 'writers' of *War Horse*, and every member of the creative team makes use of it in imagining sequences. The difficulty, of course, is narrowing down the aesthetic, and here the critical object is Captain Nicholls' drawing of Joey – the inspiration, Michael Morpurgo claims, for the original story.

The flexibility of the screen allows the team to devise a developing visual language to accompany their story. Simple line drawings using soft watercolours in Devon shift into an edgier monochrome that picks up on the modernist art movements of the period – Futurism and Vorticism, and takes their cues of fragmentation and distortion to create a nightmarish war of rough, broken, animated shadow forms moving through devastated landscapes. "There are three states in the play," says Kohler, "before the war, during the war, and after the war. And you have to make a decision on how to show that. Because after the war is not the same as before." The final return to Devon cannot be a return to the same aesthetic – the world will never be the same again for those who lived through it.

Rae Smith brings a focus on Vorticism to the table, and Handspring, Morris and Elliott feed on it. The Vorticist aesthetic invites the screen to become more than something that accompanies or illustrates the action, and tempts Handspring to push their expertise too, blending projected image, two-dimensional, and three-dimensional shadow shapes together in sequences that are enacted simply, live on stage, but transformed into truly new shadow puppetry experiments on the enormous screen. Puppetry responds well to a move away from naturalistic representation. "We are going into areas where we've never been before," says Basil Jones excitedly. FiftyNine's technical expertise is crucial here, as they work to stitch together the multiple cameras and projectors needed to fill the enormous screen, and apply time-lapse filters to the puppetry action that give the movements the same sense of lurching distortion that the visual style brings to the puppets themselves. FiftyNine are able to set up a draft version of the system in the 2007 workshop – essential for Smith, Jones and Kohler to find common ground for their ideas about this powerful area of the stage picture.

The shadow work feeds back into what's planned for the stage, too, in unexpected ways. The appearance of a First World War tank, a major challenge for Rae Smith and production manager Sacha Milroy, suddenly has a possible form of realisation – as the aesthetic of the screen invades the stage. The bold strips of the shadow puppets link both with the cane frame of the horses and with the riveted substructure of mechanised war; and the idea forms of a wholly puppet tank – a symbol, rather than a figurative representation of the roaring, groaning, staggering technological advance that confronts Joey. This idea of the tank grabs hold of all the creative team, as Sacha Milroy relates:

> What's interesting about the tank is, we've got a huge, huge object: it needs to be incredibly lightweight because we want to carry it out over the audience, and over people's heads... we thought that might not be a big problem, until [sound designer] Chris Shutt said he'd like to put a couple of speakers in it. And then [lighting designer] Paule

[Constable] said 'I'd like to put some lights in it'. So we've got a little way to go on how we solve that.

But the tank represents a continuity between the screen and stage action; and as Smith's assistant Will Fricker makes a scale model of the real tank, and someone picks it up and brings it into the shadow puppetry set-up, throwing an enormous, looming image of it onto the screen, the relationship between the worlds comes closer and closer. Vorticism slips from the screen onto the stage via developments of the design of the gun and tank – so the world of the war becomes increasingly fragmented and non-realistic – like the traumatised perceptions of the soldiers.

4. The Olivier

If you've never worked here, you've never worked on a stage like this. I think it's a fairly unique stage in the world.

Adrian Kohler

THE OLIVIER THEATRE is one of the most daunting spaces in British theatre. Nearly 1200 seats mean that a production needs to have plenty of appeal. Some have made use of its similarity to a Greek amphitheatre, with the wide curve of seating radiating from a nearly-circular stage, to emphasise speech and epic performance. Others focus the action down on to a small area of the stage, inviting the audience to lean in and imagine a smaller theatre. In recent years, the National's immensely popular £10-ticket seasons have seen productions with low design budgets manage to fill the space with ingenuity and flair. *War Horse* offers an opportunity to put some of the impressive machinery of the Olivier into action; but it also challenges the creative team to conquer its difficulties. Key to that process will be Rae Smith.

"Rae Smith I absolutely adore," says Adrian Kohler. "I see her looking at everything, she's enthusiastic about what she sees, she sort of circulates around an idea, and then crystallises it into something." The creative team's response to Rae tends to centre on her thought process. Marianne Elliott is most definite, fascinated by a collaborator who is so different from herself:

Her mind is continually shocking to me. She thinks along different routes to most people. She's not logical. She's incredibly visual, but she always thinks outside the box. Always, always, always. She knows, in her body, a lot of theatre, if you know what I mean, so she knows what she's doing when she's pushing the walls down.

Smith is a mischievous figure in the room but, as Basil Jones notes, she's also "a very modest person who never pretends to have an answer when she doesn't." And in approaching the many difficulties of staging *War Horse*, Smith works hard to find the right questions. "The most challenging thing," she says, "is that there are so many components to put together the visual language of the world." Faced with a wealth of ideas and material from the large creative team, Smith waits to sense the invisible links between ideas rather than bringing in a whole set of new ones. "It's seeing what occurs amongst the team and understanding what that will be on stage, and what that will mean for the story," she clarifies. "As designer, what you're interested in is how to give context to that story, and how to allow the visual language to seamlessly flow – as opposed to being dammed up with stupid, unnecessary ideas and things that get in the way."

This will be Marianne Elliott's second production in the Olivier after the well-received *Saint Joan*. She says that "I can't imagine doing *War Horse* in a space any smaller than the Olivier, because it's such a huge visual story."

"It's terrifying," she goes on. "It's so huge. It's not just that there's a big number of seats out there. I'm used to working in the round [at the Royal Exchange Manchester]. It's very, very natural to surround a piece of drama. If somebody starts an argument in the street, and people watch it, they form a circle. So with a piece of drama, what you need to work on most is what's happening, what are the relationships, how do they talk to each other; not where they're standing, particularly. So to work in a proscenium arch theatre, like for example the Lyttelton [the National's proscenium auditorium], you have to start thinking more in pictures, like paintings. In the Olivier, you have to think even more about how to present: the acoustics are difficult, it's a massive stage, and the audience can feel a long way away from the action."

Elliott is an enthusiast. She buries herself in the project, and when she talks about a play outside the rehearsal room, it's easy to see how completely engaged she is with it – the work is the important thing, not her. In the rehearsal room, and in a meeting, she's focused and careful, rarely the loudest person in the room, and always the one who comes in to look for the clear logical line when others are being carried away on tangents. She explains to me how she came to be excited by *War Horse*: "Tom Morris told me about this project, and it sounded completely mad. And therefore brilliant. It's pushed me to work in a different way: it's much more physical theatre than I've worked in before. Much less text-based."

As Elliott has become drawn into the styles of theatre Morris is interested in investigating, and exposed to the ideas Rae Smith and the team have been coming up with, she's become more and more excited by their potential: "I think it could be a really exciting piece of theatre. All this puppetry, the visuals on the screen, and the ideas… those are big, big thoughts." But she's not blindly committed. There's a note of caution in her tone, and the clarity and decisiveness with which she approaches her work suggest she's not one to take risks: while this production will expose her to new ways of developing material, she is very precise in her approach to composing that material for presentation. One of her challenges will be to understand and use the Olivier's unique architecture.

Production manager Sacha Milroy knows the theatre well: "It is a really tricky space to design for. There is a concept that's worked really well, which is to define the acting area, to scale it down; shows that have done that in one form or another work very well. Vocally it's better, because the centre of the stage is the best place to be heard from, and it's also better visually, and financially... If you try and fill the space, it's much trickier, in all ways, I think." Nick Hytner agrees: "It's worth knowing where it's best to play a scene. And it's best to play a scene right in the centre of the stage, and around that – around the scene, as it were – you can create a massively detailed context, if you like." But Rae Smith is determined not to "build a set on top of the space." She wants to engage with the theatre as it was designed:

> Its challenge is that it's neither a theatre-in-the-round, nor an apron stage. It's got a double perspective, particularly as you move to the back of the stage, which means that you can never treat the huge vastness of space other than as a type of landscape. As you move around the Olivier stage, the point of focus shifts, so it has a strangely unspecific focus. Most people traditionally have focused with a set in the middle of the stage, and that's how the Olivier' is used a lot of the time. We're going to use the space in a completely different way, with more focus on the revolve. It's an environment in which theatre occurs, as opposed to a set on which a play occurs.

Her recognition of the theatricality of the space is key to the way the whole production has been conceived. This is how Tom Morris talks about the theatre:

> It's a space where you can't hide the audience. I really like theatre that doesn't pretend the audience isn't there, that acknowledges the audience is there, and openly invites the them to imagine more than they're seeing. That applies to a vast range of work, from Shakespeare to puppetry, and happens to be the kind of work I like. You can't deny the presence of the audience, or the imaginative game in the Olivier, so it becomes an exciting space for me.

For Adrian Kohler, the size and shape of the stage is a benefit, as he observed when the prototype puppet was taken onto the stage: "I felt these horses galloping on this round stage needed very little dressing around them: the space fitted horses very well." On that day I went to the back of the auditorium to look from the circle. Our worries that the horses would be too big were unfounded: they looked totally natural on the Olivier's stage, and from this distance, much more readable than a human figure. Perhaps Handspring have found the ideal actor for the Olivier.

Morris' 'imaginative game' is at the heart of a theatre like this, and as he points out, is essential to the activity of an audience watching puppetry. The task for the *War Horse* team is to take on the challenges of the space and of the story simultaneously.

The Olivier is often described as an epic stage, and as Nick Stafford explains, that suits this story very well. "The war's like another character, almost. And it's such a big character, that people are involved in crucial, life-or-death decisions a lot of the time. So that takes the style of writing up into what people would generally call 'epic', for want of a better word."

He goes on to talk about what the Olivier does for the way he has to write, how every major decision has to be seen by every spectator from the best stalls seats to the rim of the circle:

Because of the span of the story, and the place that it's playing in, with puppets, you need to bury intentions less, and for the audience to know very clearly what goals the characters are setting, so they can see whether they're being achieved or thwarted. There's a sort of nakedness, it feels like, sometimes.

And as the emotions are ratcheted up, the team are aware of another danger, as Basil Jones warns:

It's really important to realise how very emotional animals as subjects are on stage. Because we could swerve into an extremely sentimental piece of theatre, which worries me: but I think it could be very exciting if we avoid that and nevertheless make something that's very affecting to the audience. I hope we can find a balance: where we're showing the emotional life of a single horse and its relationship to human beings and to other horses, without necessarily making people cry at every moment.

The desire to avoid a completely sentimental spectacle is strong: as Marianne Elliott observes of the novel, "Michael Morpurgo doesn't over-sentimentalise or over-sugar moments."

Morris and Stafford have others' experiences to draw on, of course. Morris recalls one piece of advice from Nick Hytner: to focus on pure storytelling: connecting the audience with how expectations, hopes and fears are set up and fulfilled (or not). Later, Marianne remembers another point he made – about looking for the moment in any scene that makes the next one not only possible, but necessary. The tips are all about getting the critical moments of the story to resonate with everyone in the theatre. Stafford also recalls a more informal piece of advice, from playwright Nicholas Wright (who adapted *His Dark Materials*): "He said, 'Front, Front! Get everything down the front!'"

Rae Smith's ideas, expressed on her storyboard, indicate how the story will occupy the space. But she's not able to pin down every scene. For example, the sequestering in the Devon village square, where the army are recruiting men and buying horses. There are lots of points of focus, characters constantly arriving and leaving, and multiple narratives going on. It's almost impossible to keep the bustle and excitement of the village and still direct the audience's attention to the details. Elliott, Morris and Smith have a number of possible ways to solve this, which remain active in discussion throughout rehearsals. As Jones says, "the design comes in the doing rather than in the planning. And," of Smith, as she holds back on some of these decisions, "my respect for her grows as we work together."

The space that Smith offers for storytelling is a plain and simple one. "Puppeteers and actors will tend to merge," she says. "Transforming from agricultural workers into British soldiers into German soldiers." Significantly, in discussions about the shape of the story, Smith's preoccupation is often with the large-scale movement of the ensemble of actors. Her emphasis is on the dynamic, and when she talks about using the Olivier's revolve and 'drum' elevator, it's again in terms of movement, rather than of using the machinery to reveal fixed pictures. Smith wants to employ the revolve in the way a film-maker might use a pan or dolly shot, changing the point of view on a scene – transforming it in a way that is part of the direction of the piece – and gratefully accepted by Elliott and Morris. Smith's suggestions for use of the Olivier's machinery occupy large moments – the whole stage rotating – and tiny ones: "it would be great," she says of the dead and dying Coco and Heine, "to sink them through the floor."

"She's really into atmosphere," says Elliott about Smith. "Because she understands the feeling or the mood of the scene. So does Paule [Constable, our lighting designer]." Together, Smith, Elliott and Constable focus on moving Stafford and Morris' storytelling forward, keeping the energy of the ensemble alive, and propelling it into the auditorium.

The Olivier is a big, open space: there's nowhere to hide, and Smith has made the decision not to break up its scale with scenic barriers. The visibility of the puppeteers offers a solution to creating a language of scenery that lasts only as long as the storytelling actors need it to: the doors, poles and edges of the playing space will be held and moved by human beings, just as the puppets are. The simple staves or poles that will be used relate also to the poles that the puppeteers use to control the flying birds or the horse's heads. Tom Morris relates them to a hurdle – a portable, freestanding piece of farm fencing made from lengths of natural wood. The poles offer us a link between the cane and wood of the puppets and the materials used in the scenery.

Looking at a scale model of the Olivier helps us in planning the big storytelling decisions. Moments like the opening of the play are debated time and time again, but it seems certain that the first figure the audience see should be a puppeteer with a bird, "christening the space", as Jones describes it. Plotting through scenes with the model indicates various things about the speed of storytelling that aren't evident from simply reading the script. For example, how big a deal hitching Joey up to the plough could be – and the question of where he could pull the plough to. Several moments in the story focus on horses pulling, and the Olivier's revolve will give us the necessary sense of motion without taking the action off the stage.

These considerations of design feed into the scriptwriting, and Nick Stafford is always there for these plans – every design meeting also writes a bit of the script. The physical business of ploughing must be the centre of that scene, for example, and as Stafford makes plans to alter his script to accommodate it, Morris brings up the possibility of using music in the scene too. He hazards a suggestion of Albert singing, but when composer, folklorist and long-time National Theatre artist John Tams comes to visit the workshop, the whole village sings, embodying the effort of Joey and Albert in a rousing chorus. For Morris, it's one of his defining memories:

> *The combination of puppet and song was a big eye-opening moment in the last workshop. So, I know, from my work with [director] Carl Heap – and from seeing The Mysteries here at the NT – that the use of folk song to get*

the audience to believe in a theatrical moment can work very powerfully. Actually I've yet to see that happening in the Olivier, so we may all fall flat on our faces. But I didn't understand until we did the ploughing scene with, actually, the wrong song, quite how well that would engage with the imaginative game you're playing anyway with the puppet.

And it just seemed to absolutely, naturally convince.

The music and song in *War Horse* is shared between John Tams (whose work at the National dates back to *The Mysteries* in 1977), composer Adrian Sutton (whose work in the Olivier includes the stirring musical work on *Coram Boy*), and sound designer Christopher Shutt. When he comes to watch a read-through in early 2007, Shutt makes a beeline for Rae Smith's visual research – he's another collaboration-minded artist. In the time between the final workshop and the rehearsals, the use of folk singing confirms itself as *War Horse*'s main musical strand. John Tams' approach to the singing – it's an expression of community through joy in the music, not a prim rendition of the song – links well with the production's focus on ensemble. Morris and Elliott recruit Tim van Eyken, an award-winning young star of folk, to join the company in a new character called Songman – who'll be the leader of the voices on stage.

John Tams is a substantial presence, but informal, approachable, and immensely knowledgeable. He offers us not just songs, but their context. And the context comes in stories and anecdotes – not dry 'folk' tradition but the live culture of actual folk. We hear about broom dances, guising and the mechanisation of agriculture as if he had been there. And his recall of songs is winning. "The human voice is the only instrument that can do two things at once:" he says. "It can tell you a story and it can carry a melody. No other instrument in the world can do that." And he sings.

The songs Tams teaches the company form the first point of reference for Adrian Sutton's compositions. In parallel with Rae Smith's visual journey from romantic drawings to broken futurist visions, Sutton will plot a stylistic journey from Mahler to Stravinsky – shifting from lyrical motifs into a splintered orchestral soundscape, working both with recorded music and a live band. Tom Morris is enormously enthusiastic about the music and is the first point of contact for Sutton and Tams, but here as elsewhere, his desire is to prompt rather than instruct them – indicating avenues for his collaborators to explore.

Any concerns over sentimentality are magnified whenever Sutton comes in to underscore a sequence in workshop or rehearsal. With a story with so much loss and sadness, and one which invites us to empathise with the perspective of animals, it doesn't take much to bring a tear to the eye of suggestible theatre folk. Adrian Sutton is vocal about this himself, conscious perhaps that his contribution is what could tip the balance. "It's to do with harmonic quality," he notes, and warns against a tendency to underline what is already being acted by the actors and puppeteers: "What the music must not do is to replicate what we're already seeing," he says. He's a regular presence in rehearsals, applying his latest drafts to accompany scenes, before touching heads with Morris and returning to another room in the building to make his changes. He always asks the actors to try to ignore the music he's providing – to play their own rhythm rather than joining the swell of his instruments. His impact on *Coram Boy*, working again with sound designer Chris Shutt, was enormous, and all the creative team hope that he can bring the same power to *War Horse*'s narrative.

• • •

Smith and Sacha Milroy regroup after the workshops are over to go through the 'white card model' – a sketch, for costing purposes, of the plans for the production. Milroy describes Smith's process: "She's had to tie together all the things that came out of the workshop and find a language that was influenced by Adrian and Basil. It's complicated because there are so many different people's views within the creative team to take on board, and also hard to find the time to have conversations with everybody in different places. There's a lot unknown about this show so far. There are elements we know and there are elements we don't really have enough information on, that won't come out until later… because too many people need to have conversations about what it should and shouldn't be. It's going to be easier when everybody's here." With key collaborators on another continent, and a large creative team who are often involved in other work, waiting (and emailing) becomes a big part of everyone's job.

An example of Milroy's difficulties is the screen itself. "Everybody's got a different take on it. So there's a design take on what it should look like round the outside, and whether it's got texture… and there's practicality: how to rig it and rep it, how to move such a big object. Then there's the video guys, who want a certain type of pvc on it to get the best video image, and Chris Shutt would like it acoustically permeable… but Paule would like it solid. So someone," she smiles, "is going to have to compromise a bit."

As she looks forward to the final stretch of rehearsals, Milroy is setting herself up to respond quickly as decisions are made. "What's going to be tricky," she admits, "is working out who takes a lead on which area. Because trying to have a committee of people making a decision about something is going to be really hard. Or trying to encourage people creatively to make a decision… I think that's going to be the biggest challenge, really."

The making of *War Horse* is the coming together of these many collaborators and their falling into rhythm with each other. "It's too big for one person," says Elliott. "It's too big for one ego to be bossing around. We're trying to do everything in a new way, aren't we?" And the linking together of these people is the key to the success or failure of *War Horse*: her clear, astute choices, Morris' eager experiments, Kohler and Jones' limit-pushing intricate designs and Smith's sweeping dynamics, mixed in with a little technique and detail from Sedgwick, Shutt, Constable and the rest of us. Michael Morpurgo reflects on the progress of his story:

> *I just find it enormously moving that something that started down in this little place in Devon 20-odd years ago, has attracted all these fresh minds to it, and they're creating something new, different, that tells, to a large extent, the same story, but in a different way.*

5. Soldiers and Farmers

The danger is, it might work. It might successfully tell the story of a horse having a tough time. And that might put enough grit in the cream to make it a satisfying story, but it mustn't just be about that. It has to be about what happens to people in war as well.

Tom Morris

MICHAEL MORPURGO KNOWS what he hopes for *War Horse*: "I want no-one to come out of that play – or indeed finish the book – thinking that this is about winning a war. Above everything it is about how every single side suffers." As the company approach production they need to keep this in mind, in creating the characters in the script. Morpurgo talks about the characters at the root of the story:

Most of us grow up with the First World War poets. Well the fact is this: grand and wonderful as some of these poems are, and heartrending, most of them were written by officers, who came to the war with a certain class, a certain idea, a certain notion. The people I was talking to in Iddesleigh were, if you like, the fighting men. People who came to the war straight, without verses, and thinking, and philosophy and literature to either help or hinder them: they came to it straight. And I had always wondered, with my listening to them, and my reading of history, how it was that these men did go up over the top, because people told them to do it.

"The whole farming family," Morpurgo says, "and Albert, are very rooted in the people I know and live amongst in Devon to this day. The character of Albert is not one person, but an amalgam of young boys I saw, coming home from the local comprehensive, finishing their schooling very young and going straight out on the farm: that's what was expected of them." He talks about the village of Iddesleigh, where he lives and from where he draws inspiration. In the schoolroom there you can see photographs of classes gone by, including one of the young class of 1911: "You can see the people in 1911 in their hobnailed boots, these little kids. And these are the ones who went off to war only six or seven years later. And one of those, in my head, was Albert."

The equivalent is true of the German characters – also fighting men in difficult circumstances. Morris, Elliott, Stafford and the team have been thinking about these characters for a long time, speculating and researching about their backgrounds and culture – but the actors only join *War Horse* on 13 August. The play script can't include everything about the village, the time, the Army or the war; but the story relies on these being vividly created, to breathe and emerge. There are only seven weeks to make it coherent: so how will they go about it?

Marianne Elliott has a rigorous approach. "I do weeks of prep before rehearsals begin," she says emphatically. "Weeks of it. Working out what the text is, looking at every line. You look at every single word that they say, thinking 'What does that mean? Why do they say it? Exactly for what reason? What was the word that made her respond like that?' Trying to keep the acting on the lines, so everything that character says is affected by how she feels."

And the actors go about their own research. Michael Morpurgo and Luke Treadaway, playing Albert, have already been in contact. "What's really lovely," says the writer, "is that we've arranged, with the help of the King's Troop, for the guy who is playing Albert (who comes, funnily enough, from a village just down the road), to go off and spend three or four days with them working with the horses, riding the horses, talking to the troopers, getting under the skin of this whole thing."

Before rehearsals start, every actor is requested to have read Erich Remarque's *All Quiet on the Western Front*, that most essential and vivid of war novels, and most have sought out other background material. In the rehearsal room, staff director Polly Findlay is the custodian of the research table and bombarded with requests for extra information-gathering. Books about the First World War and war memoirs by Graves and Sassoon are there of course, but also volumes on horse-training, about life in Britain before the War, about farming, and novels and poetry too – including several volumes by Michael Morpurgo. Each member of the team leaves their personal inspirations there for general inspection: so the company can leaf through Adrian Kohler's collection of images of horses, and Tom Morris and John Tams' musical references. Rae Smith has done masses of visual research and there are plenty of images, especially of the grimness of war.

The idea of an ensemble is very important to Morris and Elliott. Time and time again as rehearsals continue, they emphasise the work the company are doing to tell the story as a group. Morris has stressed throughout the workshop that it's the ensemble who have a collective storytelling responsibility to the audience; this is a show that doesn't stand or fall on one central performance, but in which the group of performers combine to create the story.

By February 2007 we knew that the company was to be 30, all of whom would work all over the stage as required. Five would be specialist musicians, twenty-five performers with skills in acting and puppetry. Nine of those, with different levels of puppetry experience, have benefited from a final workshop courtesy of the Studio: two weeks of training with the puppets immediately before rehearsals begin. As the puppetry roles are allocated finally, during the rehearsal process, these nine share their skills and insights with the rest of the company. The directors are absolutely determined that the company should come across to the audience as a united group: not 'puppeteers' and 'actors'. Rae Smith sounds very pleased when she tells me that "the audience won't be able to tell the difference between actors, puppeteers and musicians. Really." Smith, conscious that the visual picture will always include performers holding puppets, has invited them to utilise the ensemble as scenery too: walls, doors, and windows are to be 'puppeteered', and the bodies of performers will become part of the background of every scene, whether they are sending Nicholls through the air from Joey's back into his tree, or manipulating the enormous tank that threatens Joey before he tries to flee the war altogether. And Morris and Elliott have cast actors who are willing to take this work on: Angus Wright is as focused when holding a pole to help create a stable as he is carrying the main focus as Friedrich. As he says, "you do that there, and that there, and then come on here, and then I do this pole, and then I'm back to this villager, or whatever it is. But this is such a huge project that it requires everyone to do whatever is needed at that time." Every member of the company will handle a puppet at some time to create the big set-pieces that Stafford and his co-writers have dreamt up. Luke Treadaway's work on shadow puppetry or Paul Chequer helping to manipulate Nicholls from his horse, for example, may go unnoticed, but it's important to the entire company that everyone is ready to make their contribution to the whole picture.

The directors work to create a culture of ensemble from the first day. The actors talk to me about a feeling of egalitarianism, that everyone's ideas are listened to and none dismissed. There's a definite feeling of camaraderie among the group, and for many it's cemented playing Bally, or 'nine-square', a simple game of uncertain origin played on a large square marked out with tape on the floor and with a child's inflatable ball. Each player guards a square – if the ball bounces in your square you need to hit it with an upward or sideways stroke so that it next bounces in someone else's. If you're out, you go to the back of the queue and the next person comes in on the 'lowest' square. Players who manage to stay in, work their way to the centre: the square from which the ball is served, but the most hectic square of all. Bally is a great equaliser; it isn't about physical strength or even agility; it is above all simple, and sufficiently unfair that it continues to appeal no matter how bad at it you might be. It's played almost obsessively during every tea-break and for the last fifteen minutes of lunch. Some of the company keep playing at the end of the day after rehearsals finish. When fewer than nine are available, six- and four-square variants are played instead. The queue, often quite long in such a large company, provides a vocal bank of spectators and commentators.

Morris is keen on Bally himself and an enthusiast for using ensemble games and group warm-up exercises to get the company in harmony with each other. The games he leads prioritise the listening relationship between the performers, work to reduce our reliance on language and encourage us to find other ways of picking up on each others' behaviour, mood and intention. The central one of these, which he has used and developed through every *War Horse* workshop or rehearsal, is about peripheral vision.

Morris' Horse Walking begins as an ordinary exercise in spatial awareness for actors. Moving around a space, making sure that the gaps in it are filled, the actors stay in motion and roughly evenly spaced out. The inspiration for the exercise is twofold; one point is the knowledge that in horse body-language, a face-to-face relationship means confrontation; horses (unless aggressive) will avoid them. The other governing thought is the concept of herd behaviour; for a prey animal, being isolated from the herd is certain death. So Morris invites us to connect with first one, then more other people; by keeping an eye on their feet, or by keeping them in our peripheral vision, or by imagining lines linking us. The aim isn't picking up or copying the mood or movement quality of our (undeclared) group, but just staying aware of where they are. Frequently repeated, the game is never exactly the same twice, and variant phases involve walking backwards, or inviting confrontation. The rippling patterns of connection visible in the group are very exciting, as is the atmosphere of relaxed, silent concentration. Tom's spatial awareness and peripheral vision work is at the basis of everything we do, moving as horses, but also as villagers, soldiers or storytelling ensemble.

The application of Horse Walking to the horse is clear – most of a horse's field of vision is peripheral, and if the binocular field (straight ahead) is uncomfortable, the horse actors need to be able to think into this mode. For anyone in the ensemble, working to complement the people around you on stage is a key skill. But peripheral vision is especially crucial for puppeteers working on multi-operator puppets.

Basil Jones explains: "in puppet theatre, you're quite often working with two other people on one figure, and that whole phenomenon of being aware of what others are doing." It's essential for the puppeteers to co-ordinate with each other. And for all these peripherally-conscious actors, it's an interesting detail that the design of the Olivier stage is based on the range of peripheral vision an actor has at the 'point of command'.

"It's really important, as a team, to walk around a stage and talk about it, and about your feeling of what the warm and cold areas are," says Rae Smith. "Ultimately you have to know the space you're going to be in, especially in the Olivier, because… it's sort of operatic, and – it's also quite detailed." The paradoxes of the Olivier seem to be what gives it its particular challenge for actors.

Angus Wright is one of several *War Horse* actors performing *Saint Joan* on some evenings during rehearsals. "It feels quite small, actually," he observes, "when you're on the stage. But when you go out into the audience you realise actually it's big. It's really big." Marianne Elliott is conscious that to combat this, some performers and directors overplay the space: "What interests me in terms of acting," she says, "is what happens between the lines, what's subtextual, and what the unspoken thread is between people. I'm determined that you don't have to face out all the time; that just breaks the connection entirely. I'm determined that there must be another way."

Thusitha Jayasundera's principal role as Rose Narracott means that she will be playing some of the most intimate and sensitive exchanges in the play – and she is conscious of the demands of the Olivier too: "I've seen actors master a very easy expression in that theatre," she says, "and I've also seen a lot of actors strain there. There is a technique to it, quite clearly. I'm not confident I understand it," she smiles, a few weeks away from having to face an audience, "but it's there. It will add a very particular dimension to the piece once we get in there." Alan Williams, playing Arthur Warren, says "it seems to call for a certain relaxed precision."

Angus Wright's focus is on the vocal challenge of the space. Because of the large amount of underscore being used, the *War Horse* company will have their voices boosted with radio microphones. But Wright suggests that the best way to deal with these is to behave exactly as you would without them – and allow them to come in only when they're needed. In the Olivier, he says,

> *If you're facing straight out, and you're on the centre of the stage, it's not too hard to be heard – provided you hit the ends of words. But as soon as you face sideways, you really need to pitch up. I think that's the challenge of the*

Olivier: to find something real, a real sound, something that you believe in, that is also enunciated to that degree. We don't tend to speak in this day and age by using all the ends of our words, and so it can seem forced, and it can seem like you're 'performing' something. We'll be helped by being miked, but we will still need to work hard and Jeannette [Nelson, the National's Head of Voice] will help us – with hitting the ends of lines, really, and hitting the ends of words, because otherwise, way back up in the circle, you just hear the beginning of words, all through the sentence, until you're driven mad...

• • •

Seven weeks' rehearsals may seem luxurious but, charged up by their workshops, the team hit the ground running. The first task is to find out if the latest draft works – and the best way to do that with all this visual work is to get it on its feet as soon as possible. So, over the first three weeks of work, the company drive on through the play, stringing together three summaries on the last afternoon of each week. It's enough, reviewed on videotape, for Elliott and Morris to make their big decisions about shape and emphasis, but it means that some scenes have barely been looked at and others, staged hurriedly, are based on ideas that don't quite work. Their next step is to work with Nick Stafford, who's frequently available for rehearsals, to make alterations and cuts to bring down the play's length. *War Horse* the novel may be a quick one to read, but even having reduced the amount of it we're telling, the play is of a length as epic as its historical scope.

Over another fortnight, we work the scenes in closer detail towards fumbling runs of each act. The actors are being fed rewrites and edited versions of scenes throughout these first five weeks and can feel that the ground is shifting beneath their feet, making it difficult to give the directors what they want. Thusitha Jayasundera says:

> What I find useful, when I'm doing a play, is to understand the function of a particular scene, and what it gives the rest of the play. At the moment that's not very clear, because it keeps changing: the script keeps changing, the point of each scene seems to shift minutely, and it's quite difficult to gauge how to play something because you don't understand its function terribly well.

Luke Treadaway, whose responsibility it is to knit the audience's focus into an emotional story, is reeling after the first half run. But the simple scale and ambition of the project can also leave the individual actor feeling that *War Horse* is out of their hands. Tim Lewis, playing Topthorn's head and Major Callaghan, says, with a sort of transfixed, terrified enthusiasm: "It's ridiculous – the scale of it, and what has to be achieved, has a ridiculous quality." Alan Williams feels similarly dwarfed by the machinery of the storytelling:

> There's a feeling that you're around a great, exciting thing happening, like Niagara Falls melting in the spring, or something, but you've got about as much control over it as Niagara Falls melting in the spring. Someone says "then this stunning stuff is going to happen", "by and by, some brilliant things are going to occur with... some gloves and some fancy lighting..."
>
> By comparison, if you're doing a little three-hander at the Bush [a small London new-writing theatre], the set could fail to turn up and you'd be fine. You could do it in your sweater, that kind of thing. But this doesn't have that feeling at all. You're out of control. That's how you feel – Canute-like.

Jayasundera pinpoints that some of the bewilderment lies in "keeping abreast of all the different means of storytelling. There are about four different 'languages' that happen at the same time: the shadow puppetry, the puppets, the actors and the movement set-pieces. It's incredibly ambitious in trying to achieve an articulacy with all of those things happening together." The ensemble approach means that the actors don't even have the safety of retreating into the comfort of a single role and a single throughline – around their main characters, they need to fit auxiliary roles as wounded, villagers, soldiers, horses, and so on. But as Jayasundera declares, "I don't think there is another way of making this particular production achievable, than having all of us do everything. It does mean that in rehearsals, when somebody's trying to crack a nut that is quite difficult, it requires enormous patience."

Although Elliott and Morris prefer to work side by side, sometimes they need to split themselves between two rooms to keep to schedule. Often Adrian Kohler and Basil Jones are in a separate room working on the shadow and screen sequences with Leo Warner and some of the company while the rest work in the main room. And at the end of most days, there's half an hour or an hour for Kohler and Jones to work on refining the puppetry.

Speaking before rehearsals, Marianne Elliott is fascinated by the apparent differences in directing puppets from her work with actors. "With the puppet," she notes, "you just want it to reflect certain feelings, so there's no psychology behind it – well I'm sure there is, but it doesn't feel like it. If you move the hand a little bit on Emilie, or move the head a little bit, it means something. And all you've done is move the head. You could never say to an actor: 'just move your head to the left!' You could never do that." Small movements of the puppet, or changes of posture, can carry a great deal of meaning, and so it's essential that Handspring are able to spend time working on scenes after the characters' journeys through them have been agreed between actors and directors.

Working with puppetry presents other complications to the actors. For Angus Wright, whose role as Friedrich requires him to deliver monologues to Topthorn and Joey whilst hauling corpses and shackling harness, rehearsals can be especially frustrating, particularly when rewrites are still in progress. He's desperate to get 'off-book' so that he can work out the stage-management aspect of the harnesses and finally start to make connection between the lines and the physical business of relating to the horses.

Kohler speculates in advance of rehearsals that "I think the actors are going to need to acknowledge the style of the puppet work somehow. The piece can't be extremely naturalistic acting on the one side with the puppets on the other: I think there does need to be a sort of a halfway point between the two." He's talking about the minimalism of puppet movement – for each move to be expressive, there can't be too many. Basil Jones is always very conscious of the interplay between actor and puppeteer. From the first workshops he's been explaining that to be aware of the small movements of the horse it's necessary not to have too much peripheral movement from actors nearby.

But as rehearsals continue this seems to be less of an issue than we expected. Jamie Ballard isn't conscious of how he's altering his technique to accommodate the horse puppets: "I don't know if I'm not doing it right," he smiles, "but it just seems easy. Because you just *be*, and the horses are being." Angus Wright anticipates similar fluency once the scenes settle down: "It requires the actor coming to a certain pitch where there's give and take, and it can be slightly improvisatory, with noises, and the sound of the horse, and movement, and you just live with that, as you would with a real horse – rather than ignore it, just play with it."

But there may be more to discover in technical rehearsal and in previews as the actors adapt to the Olivier space and how the play is communicating with the audience. One cue is from Nick Stafford's text. As he describes it: "It's not like in the Cottesloe [the NT's studio theatre], where you can see people's eyes clearly, and pick up the vibrations clearly from small, tiny things. It's a big space. With big puppets on it. You can't have people whispering naturalism next to them." Alan Williams, starting to think ahead to these early performances, suggests that the key might be in front of them:

Adrian [Kohler] came in and he talked about puppets, and how they had to work, how everything has to be so precise in what they're doing. And I think we actors are going to have to regard ourselves as puppets: to be really clear and specific about where we're looking and what we're doing, and what it is that we are achieving with everything that we do. In a way that you don't necessarily have to be with a naturalistic script, where… things can be a little more diffuse.

The puppeteers have plenty of work to do to get to this level of detailed acting themselves. Basil Jones hopes that "what might really set this apart from other productions that use puppets would be a kind of refined emotional life of the figure on stage. One of the challenges is to show how subtly Joey responds differently to each person". Real horses don't move a great deal, and don't usually make a lot of noise. Consequently the tools we have to create these relationships are limited – breath, tension, the occasional vocalised whicker or whinny, and well-chosen use of the tail and ears. It's also critical that the actors, and directors, work to create the opportunities for the audience to register the horses' behaviour. The discipline of 'passing the ball' between performers – knowing when each is the audience focus – becomes a key skill in pacing the scenes.

Little puppet Emilie's behaviour is obviously psychologically motivated, but the horses need to be too. Of course none of us really knows what happens inside a horse's head, but the thought processes of the horses are the subject of plenty of speculation. Tom Morris proposes that horses have "impulse but not intention"; this is a different sort of acting. Finn Caldwell is an actor and puppeteer who plays the heart and front legs of Topthorn, as well as the vet, Major Martin. He says, of playing human and equine characters: "There is a big difference. Shifting in and out of being an actor on stage and being a horse instead is a different kind of experience. One of the biggest differences is the animal mind thing. I don't think they have long-term goals but in every moment, I think they do have goals." With the three puppeteers in each horse breathing together and concentrating on complementing each other's activity, they need to employ certain tricks of logic to work out how to respond to the scenes they are in. One is the 'monkeys' approach, in which the horse actors try to filter out the language of the scene by using the analogy of a person in a room with monkeys. Even if the 'monkeys' are screaming at one another, the horses can tell whether they are themselves under threat and respond accordingly. It's another way of helping to focus on peripheral vision, displayed emotion, and body language.

And the horse puppeteers find that the actors working alongside them can make it easier. Luke Treadaway, playing Albert, says "I look at them on stage and I think they pretty much convince you that they're horses – so what's left to do is convince that you're a person with a horse." Caldwell agrees, explaining also that in portraying a non-human, it can be a good thing to be naïve in their stage positioning:

The first three puppeteers are in the horse. The fourth puppeteer is the actor that's playing with it, and that doubles the reality of the horse. When someone's treating you like a horse, your conscious mind goes away, you just start being animal. And that's made much more apparent by the fact that when you're puppeteering, you're looking at the puppet, so it's much more difficult to be aware of other actors around you. Which in a weird way is probably helpful for the animals, because you have no stage awareness – it's hard to be useful, sort of actor-useful, in a bad way.

And Angus Wright looks ahead: "Hopefully the audience will get to a place where, as with really good mask work, they forget that what they are watching are puppet horses; they will know who Joey is. And I think we're all working towards that."

Having two directors can be problematic for a production, sacrificing a clear sense of what the piece will feel like in favour of a blend of skills. But the actors here are positive about Elliott and Morris' working relationship and the atmosphere they create – one where actors and directors are encouraged to try bold ideas. It's created not only by Morris' own chaotic openness but also by Elliott's gentle assurance; as Angus Wright puts it, "she's fiercely intelligent but she doesn't show it in an arrogant way at all." The room can sometimes be chaotic but the company trust that Tom and Marianne know where they're headed; Wright describes "a working environment that's a pleasure to be in and is highly creative." Jamie Ballard says that "it seems that they've definitely got their respective roles totally defined: so Marianne's text-based, and Tom's working with movement and pictures, and... whatever; they complement each other really well." Much of this is down to preparation and the long hours the directors spend together before and after rehearsals – this is no 10-6 job.

Marianne Elliott describes the appeal of co-directing: "Directors often feel on their own, or isolated, because they don't get to share their skills with any other director or see how any other director works. They're only ever in their own rehearsal room, and generally as a pack they're defensive, and neurotic, and threatened by each other – so to have an opportunity to work on something that really stretches you is brilliant." Of Morris, she says:

He thinks in a very different way from me. He is from a physical theatre world. He likes working on his feet very much, whereas I'm about prep, prep, prep, prep, prep. I would say that it's all in the prep, pretty much. If you cast it right, you've got a good piece of writing, and you prep it well, then you're pretty much there. But Tom works in the room. He works on his feet, he thinks from leftfield quite a lot – and he's wild sometimes in his thinking, but he keeps pushing the boundaries. We have a very good rapport between the two of us, you know, and understand each other, and respect each other a lot.

Morris' take is that he sets things up and Elliott makes them work: "I think that my skills in theatre are about spotting possibilities when ideas are growing. And that Marianne's skills are about being extremely decisive and brave in the late-call decisions… hopefully."

And they do need to think on their feet, and respond together when unexpected ideas emerge from the room, or sequences that seemed great on the page stutter on the floor.

Some scenes need calm but decisive responses – major restructuring of the mustering and learning to plough scenes, or the discovery of how Topthorn and Joey can relate to one another without playing them as people. The status of Nicholls after his death develops throughout the rehearsals. He's such a potent symbol, both of the honourable victims of the war and of Albert's subconscious, that everyone is aware that he could add something that lifts the war scenes above the prosaic. In the midst of script meetings, where every moment is rigorously justified, Stafford suggests that the team's desire to include ghosts might reflect "the tension between people wanting to be able to explain everything, and art – which doesn't."

"Sometimes it feels a little unreasonable to have Nicholls the ghost," he goes on. "And I think he'll end up being a presence. Because he can't influence events. But there's something about his encounter with Albert which is so powerful. If only Albert had had a different father, he might be like this. So he can't go until Joey and Albert are reunited."

And some changes are immediate and enjoyable. The character in the script called 'Taff' becomes 'Geordie' as played by Geordie actor Steve Harper. Much of the humour found in the play comes from the repetition of playing it in the rehearsal room, especially between the wordless horses and their keepers. Tim van Eyken's character, The Songman, doesn't appear in the rehearsal draft we read through on August 13; and yet his presence does a lot to shape the world of the play. This influence emerges through the rehearsals, with van Eyken, working in tandem with John Tams and Adrian Sutton, always ready to support key moments in the story with song and lead the company in swelling the simple folk melodies into ensemble chorus. Songman becomes one of the principal guides through the story and as I write, is in the process of resolving into another ghost, or a version of Albert, looking back on his experience. The songs themselves become hugely powerful during rehearsals, another way of bonding the company.

At the time this writing needs to be finished, we're still heading towards our last weeks of work and then technical rehearsal. Plenty might change. But the company, and directors, all share an optimism about *War Horse* that seems to extend beyond what success it might have as a single production. It's so ambitious that it seems to represent something bigger: for them personally, for the National, and even for the cavernous Olivier. Marianne Elliott says that if *War Horse* went well, "it would mean, one could start thinking more ambitiously about projects. The idea of taking a children's book, which is narrated by a horse, into a huge great big space like that is completely foolhardy. But if it works, it starts to open up the realm of possibilities about all sorts of things. It challenges the classical repertoire in there, which is really good… if it works."

• • •

Albert dreams that things are possible. And I think that's probably what is so strong about it being a horse: it's not only that looking at a horse makes us look at humans; it's also that there is something fairytale about it being a horse, and it's a fairytale ending in that respect, that Albert finds Joey. Which gives us hope: that wars end, and that people survive, and that…

Nick Stafford

I think I so wanted there to be, at the end of a story that was so much about loss, and destruction, and grief, I did want there to be… a feeling of redemption. That there is hope, even at the end of a war like that.

Michael Morpurgo

Cast List

Warhorse

Adapted for the stage by **Nick Stafford**
From the novel by **Michael Morpurgo**

Presented in association with **Handspring Puppet Company**

Jamie Ballard	Major Nicholls
Alice Barclay	Swallow/Emilie
Jason Barnett	Chapman Carter/Rudi
James Barriscale	Sergeant Bone/Colonel Strauss/Sergeant Fine
Simon Bubb	Captain Stewart/Soldat Schmidt
Finn Caldwell	Joey's mother, a horse/Goose/Topthorn/ Veterinary Officer Martin
Paul Chequer	David Taylor/Soldat Schultz
Tim van Eyken	Song Man
Thomas Goodridge	Young Joey/Topthorn
Stephen Harper	Joey's mother, a horse/Dr Schweyk/ Coco, a horse/Geordie
Thusitha Jayasundera	Rose Narracott/Private Shaw
Gareth Kennerley	Veterinary Officer Bright/Karl
Craig Leo	Crow/Joey
Rachel Leonard	Young Joey/Emilie
Tim Lewis	Topthorn/Major Callaghan
Tommy Luther	Joey
Mervyn Millar	Young Joey/Emilie
Emily Mytton	Paulette/Crow
Toby Olié	Swallow/Joey/Crow
Toby Sedgwick	Ted Narracott/Coco, a horse
Ashley Taylor-Rhys	Ned Warren/Heine, a horse
Luke Treadaway	Albert Narracott
Howard Ward	Sergeant Thunder/Soldat Klebb
Alan Williams	Arthur Warren/Soldat Manfred
Matthew Woodyatt	Heine, a horse/Ensemble
Angus Wright	Hauptmann Friedrich Müller

All other parts played by members of the company

Directors	**Marianne Elliott** and **Tom Morris**
Designer	**Rae Smith**
Puppet Design & Fabrication	**Basil Jones** and **Adrian Kohler**
	for Handspring Puppet Company
Lighting Designer	**Paule Constable**
Director of Movement	**Toby Sedgwick**
Music	**Adrian Sutton**
Songmaker	**John Tams**
Music Director	**Harvey Brough**
Video Designers	**Leo Warner** and **Mark Grimmer**
	for Fifty Nine Productions Ltd
Sound Designer	**Christopher Shutt**
Associate	**Mervyn Millar**
Company Voice Work	**Kate Godfrey** and **Jeannette Nelson**
Production Manager	**Sacha Milroy**
Staff Director	**Polly Findlay**
Stage Manager	**Jane Suffling**
Deputy Stage Manager	**Janice Heyes**
Assistant Stage Managers	**Ian Connop**, **Cynthia Duberry**, **Vicki Liles**
Costume Supervisor	**Johanna Coe**, assisted by **Jo Hunt**
Prop Supervisor	**Ellie Smith**
Assistants to the Designer	**William Fricker**, **Susannah Morgan**
Assistant to the Lighting Designer	**Nick Simmons**
Assistant Production Manager	**Tom Richardson**
Design Associate	**Tim Blazdell**
Production Photographer	**Simon Annand**
German translation	**Heike Roemer**
French translation	**Christopher Campbell**